CAST IRON COOKING
INSIDE & OUT

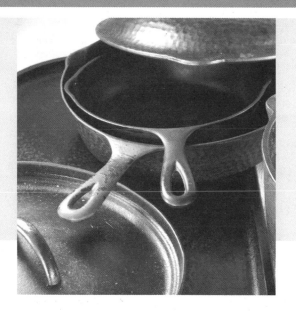

How to use this book

Each recipe offers directions for cooking inside with the stovetop and/or oven or outside on a campfire or grill (with or without a grate). Icons throughout the book show the type and size of cookware to use. Remember that weather conditions will affect cooking time outdoors, so if it is cold, windy or wet, you'll probably need more coals and extra time.

Follow this easy key to success

If it says...	It means...
24 (+) hot coals	Start with 24 hot charcoal briquettes but light extras to complete the cooking.
about 24 hot coals	You'll need about 24 hot charcoal briquettes to complete the cooking.
cook on a grate	Start with the grate 3" to 4" above heat and adjust it up or down as needed for correct cooking temperature.
medium heat	Medium setting on a gas grill or holding your palm above the fire for 4 seconds at about the position the food will cook. (2 seconds=hot heat; 6 seconds=slow heat)

Printed in the United States of America
by G&R Publishing Co.

Distributed By:

Products

507 Industrial Street
Waverly, IA 50677

ISBN-13: 978-1-56383-423-3
ISBN-10: 1-56383-423-5
Item #7072

TABLE OF CONTENTS

Cast Iron: Back to the Basics

For hundreds of years, cast iron pots have been hung over open fires and set on hot coals to simmer stews or roast meats and vegetables. Hot coals were heaped on the lids of Dutch ovens to bake delicious breads and desserts. From morning to night, the hardworking cookware turned out hot and hearty food.

When wood-burning stoves came on the scene, the shape of cast iron pots and pans changed. Legs were no longer needed to hold a pot above hot coals, so pots with flat bottoms became more effective. But the skillets, griddles and cooking pots were still cast from a piece of metal and designed to withstand high heat, frequent use and some rough handling.

With the invention of artificial nonstick materials like Teflon®, the cookware industry changed again. People wanted pots and pans that were lightweight, pretty and pre-treated for nonstick cooking. And it helped if the items could go into a dishwasher. Cast iron skillets, griddles and Dutch ovens were relegated to the back shelf in favor of the newest and "greatest" cookware available. If the cast iron pieces were lucky, they found a new home with the family camping gear.

But today, we're rediscovering something our grandparents knew all along: cast iron cookware produces mouthwatering foods, and it's durable enough to be passed down through generations of cooks. These old standbys are one-time purchases and the cooking surfaces just get better with age and regular use. With proper handling, foods practically slide out of the old cast iron pots and pans as if they had nonstick finishes – without any worry about special utensils, flaking chemical coatings or scratches that damage the finish.

Characteristics of Cast Iron Cookware

It's versatile. Made from a single piece of metal, it can go directly from stovetop to oven and be used with campfires and grills. You can brown food in a skillet and then transfer it directly into a hot oven to finish cooking. That's one-pot cooking at its best!

It's heavy. This means it's durable and will maintain an even cooking temperature once it is heated. Look for sturdy handles on both sides to make handling easier. Use both hands to lift and move pans.

It can handle high temperatures. Food will brown nicely and crusts will be crisp. But the pots and handles retain heat, so use good pot holders.

It's green cooking. Not only is cast iron cookware relatively inexpensive, it will last for generations. Buy new or shop at second-hand stores or estate sales for used cookware.

It's natural, nonstick cooking. There are no artificial chemical coatings to be concerned about – just the natural oils you use to season the cookware.

It can add an important nutrient to your food. A bit of iron leaches from the pan into the food being prepared, bumping up the iron content for your body to absorb. (Acidic foods, like tomato sauces, pull out more iron from the pans, so limit the cooking time of these foods to 30 minutes or less to avoid any metallic taste.)

Prepping & Caring for Cast Iron

To season: Cast iron must be "seasoned" to build a smooth, naturally glossy cooking surface (patina) and prepare it for nonstick cooking. Rub a thin layer of vegetable oil or shortening over all surfaces of cookware. Place the pan upside down on a rack in a 350° oven for 1 hour (with foil on the bottom of oven to catch any drips). Turn off oven and let pan cool completely. Then wipe with a paper towel. Refresh seasoning as needed on stovetop or in oven, and cook with oil periodically to build the patina.

To clean: Pans may be cleaned without water by scrubbing with coarse salt or a plastic scraper and then simply wiping with a clean rag. They may also be washed with very hot water and a stiff nylon brush or scrubber, rinsed and wiped dry. It's best to avoid dish soap (it strips off the seasoning and can seep into the metal), but if you feel it's necessary to get your pan clean, use it sparingly and then refresh the seasoning.

To dry: Wipe cookware with paper towels or old towels (cast iron can leave black stains). Then set it on a burner over low heat to remove remaining moisture and prevent rust. Periodically, lightly coat the inside of the warm pan with oil or shortening and return to low heat for 1 to 2 minutes to refresh seasoning. Let pan cool completely before storing.

To store: Store uncovered in a dry location (such as inside the oven). If rust appears, scrub it off with steel wool and reseason thoroughly.

Types of Cast Iron Cookware

Dutch oven: deep, thick-walled cooking pot with a tight-fitting lid

Camp-style Dutch oven

- primarily for outdoor cooking with a campfire

Features: 3 short legs, flat lid with a vertical lip (to hold hot coals), sturdy cast iron handle on lid, strong wire handle attached at the sides (to lift or hang pot).

Kitchen-style Dutch oven

- for indoor cooking on stovetop or in oven
- outdoor cooking on a grate or propane burner

Features: flat bottom, domed or rounded lid (it won't hold coals), sturdy handle on lid and each side, optional wire handle (to lift or hang pot)

Buying tips: Though you can purchase many different sizes, a 10" and/or 12" Dutch oven (3" to 4" deep) will be most useful for general cooking. A 10" Dutch oven can be stacked on top of a larger one during cooking to share coals and space.

CAUTIONS

- Don't put cold water into a hot pan (or hot water into a cold one) – it can crack.
- Never leave cast iron soaking in water – it may rust.
- Don't wash cast iron cookware in the dishwasher, unless you need to strip the pan to prepare it for the seasoning process.
- Cast iron holds heat, so use thick pot holders when handling pots and pans.
- Enamel-coated cast iron is not designed for outdoor cooking and requires some special care.

Skillet: heavy frying pan (1" to 3" deep), usually round, with or without a lid

- for indoor cooking on stovetop or in oven
- for outdoor cooking on a grate or propane burner

Buying tips: Though skillets come in different diameters, consider buying a small skillet (5" to 8") for sautéing vegetables and a larger skillet (10" to 12") with lid for all-purpose cooking. When purchasing larger skillets, look for an assist handle opposite the long handle to make lifting easier.

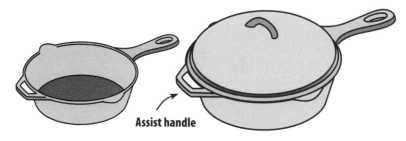

Assist handle

Griddle: large flat grilling surface with a short vertical lip around edges, usually, oblong or round

- for indoor cooking on stovetop (or occasionally, in oven) Large griddles may straddle two burners if there is space between the griddle and enameled stovetop, but limit the cooking time to avoid damage to stovetop.
- for outdoor cooking on a grate or propane burner (depending upon size)

Oblong Griddle

Round Griddle

Buying tips: Choose a size and shape that will hold the quantity of food you wish to cook at one time and one that fits on your cooking equipment. Look for a handle at both ends for easy lifting. Consider a reversible griddle with ridges on one side if you grill meat often (ridges hold meat above the heat and grease).

Cooking Inside and Out

Cooking Inside

Use the stovetop and/or oven of a standard gas or electric range and set temperatures as indicated in recipes. Cookware to use: skillets, griddles and kitchen-style Dutch ovens. If using a glass cooktop, follow manufacturer's directions and be sure the bottoms of pans are perfectly flat and smooth. Lift the cookware to move it; do not slide or drop it. To use a camp-style Dutch oven in a standard kitchen oven, straddle its three legs over the rungs of the oven rack. Pull out rack and carefully lift the pot to move it.

Cooking Outside

On a campfire, burn wood or charcoal briquettes to produce heat ("coals"), or use a gas grill with a grate or burner. Control the cooking temperatures by the number and placement of hot coals, the distance of a grate above the heat and the placement of cookware. Check food's doneness periodically and add fresh hot coals as needed to maintain the cooking temperature until food is done. Rotate cookware every 10 to 15 minutes to avoid uneven cooking or burn spots. Cooking on a grate usually requires a little extra time.

Skillets: Place a skillet on a grate directly over hot coals or gas grill heat. For a lower temperature, slide the pan to one side, away from the heat (indirect heat). Use skillets with or without a lid.

Griddles: Place a griddle on a grate directly over hot coals or gas grill heat, or move it to the side to reduce cooking temperatures (indirect heat). For griddles to perform well outside, they need even heat.

Dutch Ovens: Place a Dutch oven directly on hot coals or on a grate, or hang it over a fire. To rotate, lift pot and turn it ¼ to ⅓ turn in one direction before setting it back on heat. (Setting the legs back into vacated spaces between coals makes this easy.) Turn the lid ¼ to ⅓ turn in the opposite direction.

The number of coals you use and the way you place them will determine the cooking temperature inside a Dutch oven. Experiment with your own gear to find the methods that work best for you. The pointers on the next page will help you get started, but remember to monitor cooking and adjust the heat up or down as needed.

Dutch Oven Pointers

Camp-Style Dutch Oven (three legs): To *boil*, *fry*, *brown* or *sauté* food, use the Dutch oven without a lid. Set this pot directly on a spread or cooking ring of hot coals so all the heat comes from the bottom. The legs hold the pot slightly above the coals to avoid burning. More coals = more heat.

Spread · Ring

To *bake*, *roast* or *simmer* food in a Dutch oven, you need heat from both the bottom and top. Top heat promotes browning. Arrange some hot coals in a cooking ring underneath the covered pot and place more hot coals on the lid, either in rings or scattered evenly. For general cooking and most baking, place about ⅓ of the coals in the ring under the pot and about ⅔ of the coals on the lid. (Avoid placing any coals under the center of the pot or baked items may burn.) For roasting, split the coals evenly between the bottom and top. For simmering, place more coals underneath than on top.

Kitchen-Style Dutch Oven (flat bottom): Place this Dutch oven on a grate over hot coals (or gas grill heat) or on a gas burner.* It may also be hung over a fire on a hook or tripod by the long wire handle. To use this Dutch oven directly on hot coals, you'll need to prop it up on rocks or bricks to lift the bottom off the heat.

* A propane burner may be used like a stovetop burner.

Coals - how hot & how many?

To cook at 325°, double the diameter of the Dutch oven you're using (measured in inches) and use that number of standard charcoal briquettes.

For a 10" oven: use 20 coals (10 x 2)
For a 12" oven: use 24 coals (12 x 2)

Hotter? Every time you add two more hot coals, the temperature in the Dutch oven increases by about 25°. So to cook at 350° in a 10" pot, use about 22 coals; to cook at 400°, use about 26 coals.

Cooler? Every time you remove two hot coals, the temperature goes down by about 25°. So to cook at 300° in a 10" pot, use about 18 coals.

Where to place the coals?

If using a 12" Dutch oven with approximately 24 coals…

To sauté, fry or boil: spread all coals underneath pot (12 to 16 coals may be enough).

To simmer or stew: spread about 16 coals underneath pot and 8 coals on lid (2/3 bottom and 1/3 top). Allow coals to burn for 1 to 1½ hours before replenishing.

To roast: make a cooking ring with about 12 coals underneath pot and 12 coals on lid (½ bottom and ½ top). Replenish coals after 30 to 45 minutes or as needed.

To bake: make a cooking ring with about 8 coals underneath pot and 16 coals on lid (1/3 bottom and 2/3 top). Replenish coals after 30 to 45 minutes or as needed.

No-Count Method for Dutch Oven Cooking

If you don't want to count coals, use this quick method for any size Dutch oven: For 325° to 350°, make a ring of touching briquettes underneath the pot (leave space for legs). Make another ring of touching briquettes around the outer edge of lid. To adjust temperature up or down, add or remove coals as needed, maintaining evenly spaced rings.

Spread of coals: a flat layer of touching coals that fits underneath pot

Cooking ring: a ring of touching coals underneath pot, outer edges of coals lined up with outer edge of pot

space for Dutch oven legs

Ring(s) of hot coals on lid: one or more rings of coals around edge of Dutch oven lid (to cook from the top and promote browning)

Scattered hot coals on lid: coals placed randomly on lid

Charcoal chimney starter: tool to light charcoal briquettes more quickly

light from bottom

wadded up newspapers

Lid lifter: tool to remove Dutch oven lid without dumping hot coals or ashes into the pot

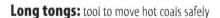

Long tongs: tool to move hot coals safely

Heavy duty pot holders/leather gloves: to protect hands when handling hot cookware

Zippy Scrambled Eggs

Serves 5

12 eggs
1 red onion
1 jalapeño pepper
¼ C. butter
Salt and pepper to taste

8 oz. firm goat cheese, crumbled
2 T. finely chopped fresh chives
Toast, muffins and/or pastries, optional

BASIC DIRECTIONS

In a medium bowl, lightly beat eggs and set aside. Finely chop onion to measure ¾ cup. Slice jalapeño into thin rounds, keeping seeds as desired. Then cook as directed on next page.

Serve
promptly with toast, muffins or pastries as desired.

COOK IT INSIDE

12"

Stovetop

Place skillet on stovetop over medium-high heat and melt butter. Add onion and jalapeño; sauté until tender. Stir in eggs and season with salt and pepper. Continue to cook and stir until soft curds form or to desired doneness. Remove skillet from heat and stir in cheese and chives.

COOK IT OUTSIDE

12"

Campfire or Grill | about 24 hot coals

Place skillet on a grate over medium heat (hot coals or gas grill) and melt butter. Add onion and jalapeño; sauté until tender. Stir in eggs and season with salt and pepper. Continue to cook and stir until soft curds form or to desired doneness. Remove skillet from heat and stir in cheese and chives.

Alternate Cooking Method

Use a griddle in place of a skillet.

Variations

• Substitute other types of cheese such as Pepper Jack, Monterey Jack or Cheddar.

• Add other diced vegetables such as bell pepper, cooked broccoli or mushrooms.

Breakfast

Shortcut Skillet Breakfast

Serves 6

1 red bell pepper, cored, seeded

1 onion

1 clove garlic

1 T. butter

2 T. vegetable oil

3 C. frozen shredded hash browns, firmly packed

¾ tsp. salt, divided

6 eggs

¼ tsp. pepper

½ C. shredded Cheddar or American cheese

¼ C. bacon bits, optional

Toast

BASIC DIRECTIONS

Dice bell pepper and onion; combine in a bowl. Mince garlic. Then cook as directed on next page.

Serve

promptly with toast.

COOK IT INSIDE

10" w/lid

Stovetop

Preheat oven to 350°. Meanwhile, place skillet on stovetop over medium heat. Add butter and oil. When hot, add bell pepper and onion; sauté until tender. Add garlic and cook for 1 minute. Stir in hash browns and ½ teaspoon salt; cover with lid and cook for 10 minutes, until potatoes are golden brown and tender, stirring often.

Remove from heat and use the back of a spoon to make six indentations in potato mixture. Break one egg into each indentation. Sprinkle eggs with pepper and remaining ¼ teaspoon salt. Reduce heat to low, cover skillet and cook for 8 to 10 minutes, until eggs are set and reach desired doneness.

Remove from heat and sprinkle with cheese and bacon bits, if desired. Cover and let stand just until cheese is melted.

COOK IT OUTSIDE

10" w/lid

Campfire or Grill   20 (+) hot coals

Place skillet on a grate over medium heat (hot coals or gas grill); add butter and oil. When hot, add bell pepper and onion; sauté until tender. Add garlic and cook for 1 minute. Stir in hash browns and ½ teaspoon salt; cover with lid and cook for 10 minutes, until potatoes are golden brown and tender, stirring often.

Remove from heat and use the back of a spoon to make six indentations in potato mixture. Break one egg into each indentation. Sprinkle eggs with pepper and remaining ¼ teaspoon salt. Cover skillet and move over indirect medium-low heat to cook for 15 to 20 minutes, until eggs are set and reach desired doneness.

Remove from heat and sprinkle with cheese and bacon bits, if desired. Cover and let stand just until cheese is melted.

Hungry Camper's Breakfast

Serves 8

1 (1 lb.) loaf white bread
12 eggs
3 T. milk
Salt and pepper to taste

1 lb. ground breakfast sausage
2 C. shredded Colby Jack cheese

BASIC DIRECTIONS

Tear or cut bread into 1" to 2" pieces; set aside. In a medium bowl, whisk together eggs, milk, salt and pepper; set aside. Then cook as directed on next page.

Do-ahead tip

Cook sausage ahead of time and refrigerate until use. Then simply grease pot with nonstick cooking spray before adding bread and other ingredients.

Serve
promtly.

COOK IT INSIDE

12"
w/lid

Stovetop & Oven

Preheat oven to 350°. Meanwhile, place Dutch oven on stovetop over medium heat; crumble sausage into pot and cook thoroughly, about 8 minutes, stirring frequently. Drain well and remove sausage to a bowl, leaving a thin coating of drippings in the pot.

Place bread pieces in Dutch oven; top with cooked sausage. Pour prepared egg mixture evenly over bread and sausage. Cover Dutch oven and transfer to center rack in oven to bake for 30 minutes.

Remove from oven, uncover and sprinkle with cheese; replace lid and return to oven for 15 to 20 minutes more.

COOK IT OUTSIDE

12"
w/lid

Campfire — 22 (+) hot coals

Arrange about ½ of the hot coals in a ring underneath Dutch oven. Add sausage and cook thoroughly, stirring frequently. Drain well and remove sausage to a bowl, leaving a thin coating of drippings in the pot.

Place bread pieces in Dutch oven; top with cooked sausage. Pour prepared egg mixture evenly over bread and sausage. Cover Dutch oven. Remove several hot coals from cooking ring underneath pot to reduce heat and transfer them to the lid; place all remaining hot coals on lid. Cook about 30 minutes, rotating pot and lid twice during cooking.

Carefully remove lid and sprinkle cheese over eggs. Replace lid and cook for 15 to 20 minutes more, replenishing coals on top and bottom as needed to maintain cooking temperature.

Variations

Add other ingredients as desired, such as sliced mushrooms, diced bell peppers or jalapeños or chopped onion.

Breakfast

Easy Breakfast Pizza

Serves 6

6 bacon strips (or sausage links, sliced)
2 green onions
3 eggs
3 T. milk
¾ tsp. salt
½ tsp. pepper
1 (8 oz.) tube refrigerated crescent rolls
3 T. diced red bell pepper
3 T. diced yellow bell pepper
1½ C. frozen hash browns, partially thawed
1 C. shredded Cheddar cheese
3 T. grated Parmesan cheese

BASIC DIRECTIONS

Cut bacon into small pieces. Slice green onions and set aside. In a medium bowl, whisk together eggs, milk, salt and pepper. Then proceed as directed on next page.

Serve promptly. Offer an assortment of fresh fruit to complement the meal, if desired.

COOK IT INSIDE

12"

Place skillet on stovetop over medium heat and add bacon; cook until crisp. Drain bacon on paper towels. Pour off grease and set skillet aside to cool. Lightly wipe out pan.

Preheat oven to 350°. Unroll crescent rolls and line the bottom of skillet with dough, pressing seams together and forming a slight rim around edge of pan. Sprinkle evenly with cooked bacon, red and yellow bell peppers, hash browns, Cheddar cheese and reserved green onion. Pour egg mixture evenly over top, keeping all ingredients inside dough's rim. Sprinkle with Parmesan cheese. Bake uncovered about 25 minutes or until crust is golden brown and eggs are set. Let cool slightly before slicing into wedges.

COOK IT OUTSIDE

12"
w/lid

Campfire | about 24 hot coals

Spread the hot coals in a flat layer underneath Dutch oven. Add bacon to pot and cook until crisp; drain bacon on paper towels. Pour off grease and set Dutch oven aside to cool. Lightly wipe out pot.

Unroll crescent rolls and line the bottom of Dutch oven with dough, pressing seams together and forming a slight rim around edge of pot. Sprinkle evenly with cooked bacon, red and yellow bell peppers, hash browns, Cheddar cheese and reserved green onion. Pour egg mixture evenly over top, keeping all ingredients inside dough's rim. Sprinkle with Parmesan cheese. Cover Dutch oven. Rearrange about ⅓ of the hot coals to make a cooking ring underneath pot; place remaining coals on lid. Cook for 20 to 30 minutes or until crust is golden brown and eggs are set. Rotate pot and lid partway through cooking and adjust the number of coals on top and bottom as needed to prevent overbrowning. Let cool slightly before slicing into wedges.

Morning Pita Pockets

Serves 6

6 medium pita bread rounds

1 onion

1 clove garlic

1 green or red bell pepper, cored, seeded

1 lb. ground sausage

12 eggs

Salsa, optional

BASIC DIRECTIONS

Slice pita rounds in half crosswise to make 12 pockets; cover until needed. Mince onion and garlic; dice bell pepper. Set all vegetables aside. In a medium bowl, beat eggs well. Then proceed as directed on next page.

Serve

promptly by spooning hot egg mixture into pita pockets and topping with salsa, if desired.

COOK IT INSIDE

Stovetop

Place Dutch oven on stovetop over medium heat; add sausage and cook until lightly browned and crumbly, stirring frequently. Add onion, garlic and bell pepper to pot; sauté with sausage until tender. Add eggs and scramble with a fork while cooking to desired doneness.

COOK IT OUTSIDE

Campfire 15 (+) hot coals

Spread the hot coals in a flat layer underneath Dutch oven. Add sausage and cook until lightly browned and crumbly, stirring frequently. Add onion, garlic and bell pepper to pot; sauté with sausage until tender. Add eggs and scramble well while cooking to desired doneness. Adjust the number of coals as needed for even cooking.

Alternate Cooking Method

Use a kitchen-style Dutch oven or large skillet and cook on a grate over medium-high heat (hot coals or gas grill).

Do-ahead tip

Brown meat and sauté vegetables ahead of time, discarding all fat; refrigerate or freeze in a zippered plastic bag. To finish cooking, add 2 tablespoons vegetable oil in place of sausage drippings and cook as directed above.

Country Sausage Gravy

Serves 10

½ onion

4 bacon strips

1 lb. ground breakfast sausage

¼ C. flour

2 C. milk

½ tsp. pepper

¼ tsp. garlic powder

Biscuits (recipes on pages 32 and 34)

BASIC DIRECTIONS

Dice onion and cut bacon into small pieces. Then cook as directed on next page.

Serve

hot gravy over biscuits or buttered toast. This gravy can also be served over mashed or fried potatoes.

COOK IT INSIDE

10"

Stovetop

Place Dutch oven on stovetop over medium heat and add sausage, bacon and onion. Cook, stirring frequently, until meat is browned and onion is tender. Do not drain off fat. Add flour and stir until blended and bubbly. Gradually whisk in 2 cups water, milk, pepper and garlic powder. Heat to simmering, but do not boil.

For thicker gravy, stir in more flour, a little at a time.

COOK IT OUTSIDE

10"

Campfire or Grill   about 20 hot coals

Place Dutch oven on a grate over medium heat (hot coals or gas grill). Add sausage, bacon and onion; cook, stirring frequently, until meat is browned and onion is tender. Do not drain. Add flour and stir until blended and bubbly. Gradually whisk in 2 cups water, milk, pepper and garlic powder. Heat to simmering, but do not boil. Adjust the number of coals as needed for even cooking.

For thicker gravy, stir in more flour, a little at a time.

Tip

To remove onion, garlic or fish odors from cast iron cookware, wipe with a little vinegar and then reseason as necessary.

Apple-Cranberry Puffed Pancake

Serves 6

1 large apple (such
  as Granny Smith)
⅔ C. flour
2 T. sugar
½ tsp. ground cinnamon
⅛ tsp. ground nutmeg
Dash of salt
4 eggs

1 C. milk
1 tsp. vanilla extract
½ C. dried sweetened
  cranberries
¼ C. butter
Powdered sugar
Maple or berry syrup,
  optional

BASIC DIRECTIONS

Peel, core and thinly slice apple; set aside. In a medium bowl, mix flour, sugar, cinnamon, nutmeg and salt. In another bowl, whisk together eggs, milk and vanilla to blend. Add egg mixture to flour mixture and whisk until smooth. Stir in cranberries. Then cook as directed on next page.

Serve

warm or at room temperature,
drizzled with syrup, if desired.

COOK IT INSIDE

10"

Oven

Preheat oven to 425°. Place butter in skillet and set skillet on center rack in oven until butter is melted. Remove skillet from oven and brush butter over bottom and sides of pan. Arrange apple slices over butter and return skillet to oven for 5 minutes or until apples begin to soften.

Pour prepared batter over apples. Bake uncovered for 18 to 20 minutes or until puffed and golden brown around edges and set in center. Cool slightly before sprinkling with powdered sugar. Cut into wedges to serve.

COOK IT OUTSIDE

10" w/lid

Campfire | **about 30 hot coals**

Arrange about ⅓ of the hot coals in a cooking ring underneath Dutch oven. Place butter in pot. When melted, brush over bottom and sides of pot. Arrange apple slices over bottom and cover Dutch oven with lid; cook for 5 minutes or until apples begin to soften.

Pour prepared batter over apples. Cover and place remaining hot coals on lid. Bake for 15 to 25 minutes or until puffed and golden brown around edges and set in center. Rotate pot and lid once during cooking and adjust the number of coals on top and bottom as needed for even heat. Cool slightly before sprinkling with powdered sugar. Cut into wedges to serve.

Variation

Mix 3 tablespoons sugar with ½ teaspoon ground cinnamon and sprinkle on top of batter before baking.

Filled Pancake Roll-Ups

Serves 6

1½ C. milk
3 eggs
½ tsp. vanilla extract
1 C. flour
¼ tsp. salt
1 tsp. sugar
Butter

Sweet or savory fillings as desired (berries, jam, diced ham, cooked sausage, shredded cheese and/or cooked vegetables)

Whipped cream, flavored syrup, honey or salsa, optional

BASIC DIRECTIONS

In a large bowl, whisk together milk, eggs and vanilla. Add flour, salt and sugar, blending until smooth. Then cook as directed on next page.

Serve

promptly, garnished with whipped cream, syrup, honey or salsa, if desired.

COOK IT INSIDE

10"

Stovetop & Oven

Preheat oven to 200°. Meanwhile, place skillet on stovetop over medium-high heat and melt 1 to 2 teaspoons butter; spread evenly over bottom of pan. Pour ¼ cup prepared batter into skillet and tilt pan so batter spreads out thinly and evenly. Cook until top looks dry, about 30 seconds. Carefully flip pancake with a spatula and cook on other side for several seconds, until golden brown.

Repeat to make additional pancakes with remaining batter. Place prepared pancakes on a cookie sheet and cover with foil; place in oven to keep warm.

COOK IT OUTSIDE

10"

Campfire or Grill   about 20 hot coals

Place skillet on a grate over medium heat (hot coals or gas grill) and melt 1 to 2 teaspoons butter; spread evenly over bottom of pan. Pour ¼ cup prepared batter into skillet and tilt pan so batter spreads out thinly and evenly. Cook until top looks dry, about 30 seconds. Carefully flip pancake with a spatula and cook on other side for several seconds, until golden brown. Adjust the number and placement of coals as needed for even cooking.

Repeat to make additional pancakes with remaining batter. Wrap pancakes in foil and set over indirect heat to keep warm.

Alternate Cooking Method

Use a griddle in place of a skillet. Spread out batter with a large spoon.

Hearty Cornmeal Pancakes

Serves 4

½ C. flour
½ C. whole wheat flour
½ C. cornmeal
2 T. sugar
1¼ tsp. baking powder
½ tsp. baking soda
1 tsp. salt

1½ C. buttermilk
¼ C. milk
3 T. butter, melted
   and cooled
1 egg, lightly beaten
Additional butter
Syrup (recipes follow)

BASIC DIRECTIONS

In a medium bowl, stir together flour, whole wheat flour, cornmeal, sugar, baking powder, baking soda and salt. In a separate bowl, whisk together buttermilk, milk, melted butter and egg. Whisk milk mixture into dry ingredients until just combined (lumps will remain). Then cook as directed on next page.

Serve
   with warm syrup.

COOK IT INSIDE

Griddle

Stovetop & Oven

Preheat oven to 200°. Meanwhile, place griddle on stovetop over medium heat. When hot, grease lightly with butter. Spoon ⅓ cup prepared batter onto griddle for each pancake. Cook until edges are set, 3 to 4 minutes (bubbles will not appear as with traditional pancakes). Flip pancakes and cook until golden brown, about 2 minutes.

Repeat with remaining batter, greasing griddle as needed. Keep prepared pancakes warm on a cookie sheet in the oven.

COOK IT OUTSIDE

Griddle

Campfire or Grill | about 20 hot coals

Place griddle on a grate over medium heat (hot coals or gas grill). When hot, grease lightly with butter. Spoon ⅓ cup prepared batter onto griddle for each pancake. Cook until edges are set, 3 to 4 minutes (bubbles will not appear as with traditional pancakes). Flip pancakes and cook until golden brown, about 2 minutes. Adjust the number and placement of coals as needed for even cooking.

Repeat with remaining batter, greasing griddle as needed. Stack cooked pancakes on aluminum foil, cover lightly and set over indirect heat to keep warm.

Try these syrups

Maple Syrup: In a small pot over medium heat, mix 1 cup brown sugar, 1 cup sugar and 1 cup water; boil until sugar dissolves. Remove from heat and stir in ¼ cup light corn syrup, 1 teaspoon each of maple and butter flavoring and ½ teaspoon vanilla.

Honeyed-Orange Syrup: Zest and juice one orange. In a small pot over medium heat, mix 1 cup honey with juice; bring to a boil, stirring constantly. Remove from heat and stir in zest.

French Toast Bake

Serves 6

1 (1 lb.) loaf French bread
¼ C. butter
8 eggs
3 C. milk
¼ C. sugar

1 tsp. ground cinnamon
¾ tsp. salt
1 tsp. vanilla extract
Maple syrup, optional

BASIC DIRECTIONS

Tear bread into 1" to 2" chunks. Cut butter into small pieces; set aside. In a medium bowl, whisk together eggs, milk, sugar, cinnamon, salt and vanilla until blended. Then proceed as directed on next page.

Serve
promptly with syrup.

COOK IT INSIDE

Oven — 12" w/lid

Preheat oven to 325°. Lightly grease Dutch oven with nonstick cooking spray. Place bread chunks in pot. Pour prepared egg mixture over bread, stirring lightly to mix. Scatter set-aside pieces of butter over top. Bake uncovered for 30 to 40 minutes or until set.

COOK IT OUTSIDE

Campfire — **24 (+) hot coals** — 12" w/lid

Lightly grease Dutch oven with nonstick cooking spray. Place bread chunks in pot. Arrange about ⅓ of the hot coals in a ring underneath Dutch oven. Pour prepared egg mixture over bread, stirring lightly to mix. Scatter set-aside pieces of butter over top and cover pot with lid.

Place remaining hot coals on lid and bake for 30 to 45 minutes or until set. Rotate pot and lid several times during cooking and replenish coals on top and bottom as needed to maintain cooking temperature.

Variations

Quick French Toast Bake: Replace milk and seasonings in recipe with 3 cups eggnog and prepare as directed.

Blueberry French Toast Bake: Soak bread chunks in milk mixture for 20 minutes. Add 2½ cups fresh blueberries and a splash of vanilla extract; toss well. Pour into Dutch oven and dot with butter. Bake as directed.

Griddle French Toast: Cut milk and egg mixture in half. Slice bread and soak slices in milk mixture briefly. Fry on griddle until golden brown on both sides.

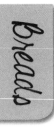

Breads

Buttermilk
Biscuits

Serves 10

2 C. flour
¾ tsp. salt
½ tsp. sugar
1 T. baking powder
½ tsp. baking soda

5 T. butter, sliced
1 C. buttermilk
Butter, jam, honey and/or
sausage gravy

BASIC DIRECTIONS

In a large bowl, mix flour, salt, sugar, baking powder and baking soda. With a pastry blender or two knives, cut in butter until mixture is crumbly. Add buttermilk and stir until dough holds together.

Place dough on a well-floured surface and knead lightly several times. Flatten dough with hands or rolling pin to 1" thickness. Cut biscuits with round cookie cutter, drinking glass or empty soup can from which both ends have been removed. Then bake as directed on next page.

Serve

warm or at room temperature with butter, jam and/or honey as desired, or slice and serve hot with Country Sausage Gravy (recipe on page 22).

COOK IT INSIDE

12"

Oven

Preheat oven to 375°. Grease bottom of skillet with nonstick cooking spray. Arrange biscuits in a single layer in skillet and bake uncovered for 15 to 20 minutes or until golden brown.

COOK IT OUTSIDE

12"
w/lid

Campfire | about 28 hot coals

Grease bottom of Dutch oven with nonstick cooking spray. Arrange about ⅓ of the hot coals in a cooking ring and set Dutch oven on top for 10 minutes to preheat.

Arrange biscuits in a single layer in Dutch oven. Cover pot and place remaining hot coals on lid. Cook for 15 to 25 minutes or until biscuits are golden brown. Rotate pot and lid twice during cooking and transfer most of the hot coals from bottom ring to lid toward end of cooking time to promote browning on top.

Tip

Brush tops of warm baked biscuits with butter for added flavor.

Yam Biscuits with a Kick

Serves 10

2¼ C. flour
1 T. baking powder
1 tsp. salt
1 tsp. sugar
¼ tsp. chili powder, or to taste
⅛ tsp. cayenne pepper, or to taste

½ C. butter, sliced
½ C. drained, mashed canned yams*
¾ C. buttermilk or half & half
Butter and/or honey, optional

* You may substitute mashed baked sweet potato flesh for the canned yams.

BASIC DIRECTIONS

In a medium bowl, mix flour, baking powder, salt, sugar, chili powder and cayenne pepper. With a pastry blender or two knives, cut in butter until mixture is crumbly. Stir in yams and buttermilk until dough holds together.

Place dough on a well-floured surface and knead lightly several times. Roll out dough to ¾" thickness. Cut biscuits with round cookie cutter, drinking glass or empty soup can from which both ends have been removed. Then bake as directed on next page.

Serve

warm or at room temperature with butter and/or honey as desired.

COOK IT INSIDE

12"

Oven

Preheat oven to 400°. Generously grease bottom of skillet with nonstick cooking spray. Arrange biscuits close together in a single layer in skillet. Bake uncovered for 18 to 23 minutes or until golden brown.

COOK IT OUTSIDE

12" w/lid

Campfire — about 30 hot coals

Generously grease bottom of Dutch oven with nonstick cooking spray. Arrange about ⅓ of the hot coals in a cooking ring and set Dutch oven on top for 10 minutes to preheat.

Arrange biscuits in a single layer in Dutch oven. Cover pot and place remaining hot coals on lid. Cook for 15 to 20 minutes or until biscuits are golden brown. Rotate pot and lid once during cooking and transfer most of the hot coals from bottom ring to lid toward end of cooking time to promote browning on top.

Tip

Rotating the Dutch oven pot and lid is especially important when baking breads. It promotes even browning and prevents burn spots.

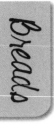

Italian Garlic Rolls

Serves 12

1 (16 oz.) pkg. Pillsbury Hot Roll Mix

2 T. plus ¼ C. butter, softened, divided

1 egg

⅔ C. grated Parmesan cheese

1½ tsp. garlic powder

2 tsp. Italian seasoning

½ tsp. dried oregano

Flour for kneading

BASIC DIRECTIONS

Following directions on roll mix package, mix contents of box and yeast in a large bowl. Stir in 1 cup hot water, 2 tablespoons butter and egg until dough forms. On floured surface, shape dough into a ball and knead until smooth, about 5 minutes. Cover dough with large bowl and let rest 5 minutes. Meanwhile, in a small bowl, stir together Parmesan cheese, garlic powder, Italian seasoning and oregano; set aside.

Roll dough into an 8 x 18" rectangle. Spread remaining ¼ cup butter over dough. Sprinkle evenly with cheese mixture. Starting at one long edge, roll up dough cinnamon roll fashion and pinch long edge to seal. Cut into rolls about 1½" thick. Then proceed as directed on next page.

Cutting tip

Use thread or unflavored dental floss to slice rolls easily and maintain round shape.

Serve
warm or at room temperature.

COOK IT INSIDE

Oven  **12"**

Grease bottom and lower sides of Dutch oven with nonstick cooking spray. Arrange rolls in a single layer in pot; cover with a cloth and let rise in a warm place until doubled in size, 30 to 40 minutes.

Preheat oven to 350°. Remove cloth and bake uncovered for 25 to 30 minutes or until lightly browned. Allow rolls to cool in pan for several minutes before removing.

Alternate Cooking Method

This recipe may also be baked in a 12" cast iron skillet.

COOK IT OUTSIDE

Campfire | **about 26 hot coals** **12" w/lid**

Grease bottom of Dutch oven with nonstick cooking spray and arrange rolls in a single layer in pot. Cover with lid and let rise in a warm place until doubled in size, 30 to 40 minutes.

Arrange about ⅓ of the hot coals in a cooking ring underneath Dutch oven and place remaining hot coals on lid. Cook for 18 to 25 minutes or until lightly browned. Rotate pot and lid twice during cooking and transfer most of the hot coals from bottom ring to lid toward end of cooking time to promote browning on top. Allow rolls to cool in pan for several minutes before removing.

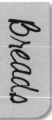

Sweet Dutch Oven Cornbread

Serves 8

1 C. cornmeal	2 eggs, lightly beaten
1 C. flour	1½ C. buttermilk
½ C. sugar	½ C. butter, melted
¼ tsp. baking soda	Vegetable oil
1 T. baking powder	Butter, jam, jelly
1 tsp. salt	and/or honey

BASIC DIRECTIONS

In a medium bowl, stir together cornmeal, flour, sugar, baking soda, baking powder and salt. In another bowl, whisk together eggs and buttermilk. Add buttermilk mixture to cornmeal mixture and stir until blended. Stir in melted butter. Then cook as directed on next page.

Serve wedges with butter, jam, jelly and/or honey.

COOK IT INSIDE

10"

Oven

Preheat oven to 400°. Brush bottom and lower sides of Dutch oven with oil. Spread prepared batter in Dutch oven and bake uncovered for 20 to 25 minutes or until lightly browned and firm in center. Let cool slightly before removing to a plate. Slice in wedges to serve.

Alternate Cooking Method

This recipe may also be baked in a 10" cast iron skillet.

COOK IT OUTSIDE

10" w/lid

Campfire   about 26 hot coals

Brush bottom and lower sides of Dutch oven with oil. Arrange about ⅓ of the hot coals in a cooking ring and set Dutch oven on top for several minutes to preheat.

Spread prepared batter in hot pot. Cover and place remaining hot coals on lid. Bake for 15 to 25 minutes or until lightly browned and firm in center. Rotate pot and lid twice during cooking and transfer several coals from bottom ring to lid toward end of cooking time to promote even browning. Let cool slightly before removing to a plate. Slice in wedges to serve.

Breads

Skillet-Baked Southern Cornbread

Serves 8

2 C. cornmeal
½ C. flour
1 tsp. baking powder
1 tsp. salt
1 egg, lightly beaten

2 C. buttermilk
3 T. warm bacon drippings
   (or vegetable oil), divided
Butter and/or honey

BASIC DIRECTIONS

In a medium bowl, stir together cornmeal, flour, baking powder and salt; set aside. In another bowl, whisk together egg, buttermilk and 2 tablespoons bacon drippings. Pour buttermilk mixture into cornmeal mixture and stir to blend. Then cook as directed on next page.

Serve
warm or at room temperature with butter and/or honey.

COOK IT INSIDE

10"

Oven

Preheat oven to 400°. Place remaining 1 tablespoon bacon drippings in skillet and set skillet in oven for 2 to 3 minutes until sizzling. Remove skillet from oven and swirl pan to coat bottom and sides.

Spread prepared batter in hot skillet and return to oven; bake uncovered for 20 to 25 minutes or until cornbread is lightly browned and pulls away from sides of skillet. Cool slightly before removing from pan. Slice into wedges.

COOK IT OUTSIDE

10" w/lid

Campfire or Grill | about 26 hot coals

Place a grate over medium-high heat (hot coals or gas grill). Place remaining 1 tablespoon bacon drippings in skillet and set on grate to preheat. When sizzling, swirl skillet to coat bottom and sides.

Spread batter in hot skillet; partially cover with lid. Spread out about ½ of the hot coals and push remaining coals to one side, or move skillet over indirect heat. Cook until top is dry, bottom is lightly browned and bread is set, about 25 minutes. Rotate skillet several times for even heat. Remove cover and carefully flip cornbread over in skillet; cook uncovered about 10 minutes more or until lightly browned on other side. Cool slightly before removing from skillet. Slice into wedges.

Alternate Cooking Method

Use a 10" camp-style Dutch oven on a ring of hot coals, with ⅔ of the coals on the lid. No flipping required.

Variations

Stir bacon bits, chopped jalapeños, hot sauce or cayenne pepper into batter before baking to kick up the flavor.

Light Monkey Bread

Serves 8

2 (7.5 oz.) tubes refrigerated country-style biscuits

3 T. butter

⅓ C. brown sugar

1 tsp. ground cinnamon

⅓ C. honey roasted sliced almonds, optional

BASIC DIRECTIONS

Remove biscuits from tubes. With kitchen shears, cut each biscuit into four equal pieces. Then proceed as directed on next page.

Serve while warm and sticky!

COOK IT INSIDE

10"

Stovetop & Oven

Preheat oven to 375°. Meanwhile, place skillet on stovetop over medium-low heat. Add butter and stir until melted. Stir in brown sugar and cinnamon until blended; remove skillet from heat.

Add biscuit pieces to sugar mixture and toss until well coated. Arrange pieces evenly in skillet. Sprinkle almonds on top, if desired. Place skillet on center rack in oven and bake uncovered for 10 to 15 minutes or until lightly browned. Let cool 1 minute and then carefully invert biscuits onto a lightly greased platter.

COOK IT OUTSIDE

10" w/lid

Campfire or Grill | about 22 hot coals

Arrange about ⅓ of the hot coals in a cooking ring underneath Dutch oven. Add butter and stir until melted. Stir in brown sugar and cinnamon until blended; remove pot from heat.

Add biscuit pieces to sugar mixture and toss until well coated. Arrange pieces evenly in bottom of Dutch oven. Sprinkle almonds on top, if desired. Cover pot with lid. Return Dutch oven to cooking ring and place remaining hot coals on lid. Cook for 10 to 17 minutes or until lightly browned. Rotate pot and lid once during cooking and adjust the number of coals on top and bottom as needed for even cooking. Let cool 1 minute and then carefully invert biscuits onto a lightly greased platter.

Alternate Cooking Method

Use a 10" skillet with lid and cook on a grate over medium heat (hot coals or gas grill). Rotate skillet twice during cooking and reduce heat as needed to prevent overcooking.

Camper's Focaccia

Serves 8

3 C. flour

2 tsp. yeast

1 tsp. sugar

3 to 4 tsp. dried herbs (such as basil, rosemary, thyme, dill or desired combination), divided

¼ C. olive oil, divided

1½ T. lemon juice

2 tsp. coarse sea salt, or to taste, divided

⅓ C. grated Asiago, Parmesan or Romano cheese

BASIC DIRECTIONS

In a medium bowl, mix flour, yeast and sugar. Add ¾ cup plus 2 tablespoons very warm water and stir until dough forms. Cover bowl and let rest for 15 to 20 minutes.

To dough in bowl, add 2 teaspoons herbs, 2 tablespoons olive oil, lemon juice, 1 teaspoon salt and Asiago cheese. Use hands to work ingredients into dough until well incorporated (dough will seem oily). Knead dough for 10 minutes until smooth. Cover with a cloth and let rise in a warm place until doubled in size, about 30 minutes. Then proceed as directed on next page.

Serve

warm or at room temperature.

COOK IT INSIDE

10"

Oven

Preheat oven to 450°. Grease skillet with nonstick cooking spray. Pat dough evenly over bottom of skillet. With fingers, press ½"-deep indentations evenly spaced over top of dough. Brush dough with remaining 2 tablespoons oil and sprinkle with remaining 1 to 2 teaspoons herbs and 1 teaspoon salt.

Place skillet on center rack in oven and bake uncovered for 15 to 20 minutes or to desired crustiness. Cool slightly before cutting into wedges.

COOK IT OUTSIDE

10" w/lid

Campfire | **about 28 hot coals**

Grease bottom of Dutch oven with nonstick cooking spray. Pat dough evenly over bottom of pot. With fingers, press ½"-deep indentations evenly space over top of dough. Brush with remaining 2 tablespoons oil and sprinkle with remaining 1 to 2 teaspoons herbs and 1 teaspoon salt. Cover pot with lid.

Arrange about ⅓ of the hot coals in a cooking ring underneath Dutch oven. Place remaining hot coals on lid. Bake for 10 to 20 minutes or to desired crustiness. Rotate pot and lid twice during cooking and check several times to monitor browning. Adjust the number of hot coals on top and bottom as needed for even cooking. Cool slightly before cutting into wedges.

Easy Sourdough Bread

Serves 12

2 C. plain yogurt	2 tsp. salt
1 T. yeast	1 T. vegetable oil
2 T. honey	4⅓ to 5 C. flour

BASIC DIRECTIONS

Heat yogurt until just lukewarm. In a large bowl, combine ¼ cup very warm water with yeast; stir to dissolve. Stir in yogurt, honey, salt, oil and 2 cups flour until blended and then beat until smooth. Gradually stir in most of remaining flour, a little at a time, adding just enough to make a soft dough that pulls away from side of bowl. Turn out on a floured surface and knead until smooth and elastic, about 10 minutes.

Place dough in a large greased bowl, turning once to grease the top. Cover with a cloth and let rise in a warm place until doubled in size, about 1½ hours. Punch dough down and shape into a round loaf. Then proceed as directed on next page.

Serve
warm or at room temperature.

COOK IT INSIDE

Oven — 10"

Grease Dutch oven with nonstick cooking spray. Place shaped dough in pot, cover with a cloth and let rise in a warm place for 45 minutes.

Preheat oven to 375°. Remove cloth and place pot on center rack in oven. Bake uncovered for 10 minutes; then reduce heat to 350°. Bake 30 to 35 minutes more or until bread is golden brown and sounds hollow when tapped. Remove from Dutch oven and cool before slicing.

COOK IT OUTSIDE

Campfire — **24 (+) hot coals** — 10" w/lid

Grease Dutch oven with nonstick cooking spray. Place shaped dough in pot, cover with lid and let rise in a warm place for 45 minutes.

Arrange about ⅓ of the hot coals in a cooking ring underneath Dutch oven. Place remaining hot coals on lid. Bake for 40 to 45 minutes or until bread is golden brown and sounds hollow when tapped. Rotate pot and lid several times during cooking and replenish coals as needed to maintain cooking temperature. To promote browning on top, transfer most of the hot coals from bottom ring to lid toward end of cooking time. Remove from Dutch oven to cool before slicing.

Tip

If desired, make several diagonal slashes in the top of the loaf before baking.

Jumbo Garlic Bread Ring

Serves 16

½ C. grated Parmesan cheese
1 tsp. garlic powder
½ tsp. onion salt

2 (1 lb.) loaves frozen bread dough, thawed until soft but still cold
⅓ C. butter, melted

BASIC DIRECTIONS

In a small bowl, mix Parmesan cheese, garlic powder and onion salt. Spread mixture on a large jelly roll pan and set aside.

Cut each loaf into four even pieces (total of eight). Use hands to stretch and form each piece into a rope about 18" long. Then proceed as directed on next page.

Serve
warm or at room temperature.

COOK IT INSIDE

Oven — 12"

Grease Dutch oven with nonstick cooking spray. Brush all sides of a dough rope with melted butter; roll in set-aside cheese mixture to coat. Coil rope in the center of pot. Continue to coat ropes, attaching to end of previous rope to form a 10" to 11" dough circle. Cover with a cloth and let rise in a warm place until doubled in size, 30 to 40 minutes.

When ready to bake, preheat oven to 350°. Remove cloth and bake uncovered for 30 to 35 minutes or until golden brown. Cool slightly before removing from pot.

COOK IT OUTSIDE

Campfire | **about 27 hot coals** — 12" w/lid

Grease Dutch oven with nonstick cooking spray. Brush all sides of a dough rope with melted butter; roll in set-aside cheese mixture to coat. Coil rope in the center of pot. Continue to coat ropes, attaching to end of previous rope to form a 10" to 11" dough circle. Cover with lid and let rise in a warm place until doubled in size, 30 to 40 minutes.

When ready to cook, arrange about ⅓ of the hot coals in a cooking ring underneath Dutch oven. Place remaining hot coals on lid. Cook for 25 to 35 minutes or until golden brown. Rotate pot and lid twice during cooking and transfer several coals from bottom ring to lid toward end of cooking time to promote browning. Cool slightly before removing from pot.

Variation

Jumbo Cinnamon Bread Ring: In place of cheese mixture, mix ½ cup sugar, ½ cup brown sugar and 1½ teaspoons cinnamon. Brush dough ropes with melted butter; roll in sugar mixture. Line Dutch oven with parchment paper. Coil coated dough ropes in pot; sprinkle with ½ cup chopped nuts. Let rise and bake as directed above. Cool slightly and frost with powdered sugar glaze.

49

Pumpkin Bread

Serves 30

½ C. brown sugar
½ C. chopped nuts
½ C. quick-cooking rolled oats
1 tsp. vanilla extract
2 T. butter
3⅓ C. flour
½ tsp. baking powder
1 tsp. baking soda

1½ tsp. salt
1 tsp. ground cinnamon
1 tsp. ground nutmeg
1 tsp. ground cloves
2 C. sugar
1 (15 oz.) can pumpkin
1 C. vegetable oil
4 eggs, lightly beaten

BASIC DIRECTIONS

In a medium bowl, combine brown sugar, nuts, oats, vanilla and butter. Mix until topping is crumbly.

In a large bowl, stir together flour, baking powder, baking soda, salt, cinnamon, nutmeg, cloves and sugar. Add ½ cup water, pumpkin, oil and eggs; mix batter well. Then proceed as directed on next page.

Serve
at room temperature.

COOK IT INSIDE

Oven

Preheat oven to 325°. Grease Dutch oven with nonstick cooking spray. Pour batter into pot and sprinkle with prepared topping. Bake uncovered for 45 to 55 minutes or until bread tests done with a toothpick. Let cool before slicing.

COOK IT OUTSIDE

Campfire   **24 (+) hot coals**

Grease Dutch oven with nonstick cooking spray. Arrange about ⅓ of the hot coals in a cooking ring and set pot on coals to preheat for 5 to 10 minutes. Pour batter into hot Dutch oven and spread evenly; sprinkle with prepared topping.

Cover pot and place remaining hot coals on lid. Bake for 40 to 50 minutes or until bread tests done with a toothpick. Rotate pot and lid several times during cooking and replenish coals on top and bottom as needed to maintain cooking temperature. Let cool before slicing.

Variation

Add 2 cups chocolate chips to batter before baking.

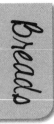

Butterscotch Pecan Rolls

Serves 24

½ C. butter
½ C. brown sugar
1 (3.5 oz.) pkg. cook & serve
    pudding mix (not instant)

24 frozen unbaked
    dinner rolls
½ C. chopped pecans

BASIC DIRECTIONS

In a small saucepan, combine butter, brown sugar and pudding mix. Then proceed as directed on next page.

Serve
while warm and gooey!

COOK IT INSIDE

Stovetop & Oven

12"

Grease bottom of Dutch oven with nonstick cooking spray. Line bottom with a circle of parchment paper and spray paper. Arrange rolls in a single layer in pot; set aside.

Place saucepan on stovetop over medium-low heat and bring pudding mixture to a boil, stirring constantly until syrup forms. Pour syrup evenly over rolls. Sprinkle with pecans. Cover pot with a cloth and allow rolls to thaw and rise in a warm place until doubled in size, 3 to 5 hours.

When ready to bake, preheat oven to 350°. Remove cloth and bake rolls for 25 to 30 minutes or until well browned and cooked through.

Let cool for 3 minutes and then carefully invert hot rolls onto a lightly greased heat-proof platter. Cool slightly before serving.

COOK IT OUTSIDE

Campfire   10+ about 26 hot coals

12" w/lid

Generously grease bottom of Dutch oven with nonstick cooking spray. Line bottom with a circle of parchment paper and spray paper. Arrange rolls in a single layer in pot; set aside.

Place saucepan on a grate over 10 hot coals and bring pudding mixture to a boil, stirring constantly until syrup forms. Pour syrup evenly over rolls. Sprinkle with pecans. Cover pot with lid and allow rolls to thaw and rise in a warm place until doubled in size, 3 to 5 hours.

When ready to cook, remove grate. Arrange about ⅓ of the 26 hot coals in a cooking ring underneath covered Dutch oven. Place remaining hot coals on lid. Cook for 25 to 35 minutes or until well browned and cooked through. Rotate pot and lid twice during cooking and adjust the number of coals on top and bottom as needed for even cooking.

Remove lid and let cool for 3 minutes. Carefully invert hot rolls onto a lightly greased heat-proof platter. Cool slightly before serving.

Quick-Fix Breads

COOK IT OUTSIDE

10"-12"
w/lid

Campfire | about 28 hot coals

Refrigerated Biscuit Dough (1 tube)

Prepare riser in Dutch oven (figure 1). Grease an 8" round metal baking pan with nonstick cooking spray and arrange biscuits in a single layer in pan. Set pan on riser and cover pot with lid. Arrange about ⅓ of the hot coals in a cooking ring underneath Dutch oven and spread remaining hot coals on lid. Bake about 10 minutes or until golden brown.

COOK IT INSIDE

8"

Oven

Frozen Dinner Rolls (8 to 10 rolls)

Grease skillet with nonstick cooking spray. Place frozen rolls in skillet, cover with greased waxed paper and set in a warm place to rise, 3 to 5 hours. When doubled in size, preheat oven to 350° and bake rolls for 15 to 20 minutes or until golden brown.

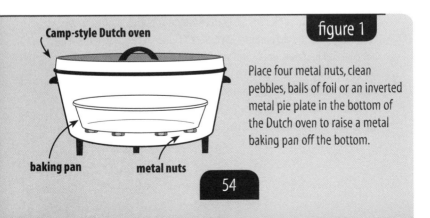

Camp-style Dutch oven

figure 1

Place four metal nuts, clean pebbles, balls of foil or an inverted metal pie plate in the bottom of the Dutch oven to raise a metal baking pan off the bottom.

baking pan   metal nuts

COOK IT INSIDE

8"

Packaged Cornbread Mix (1 package)

Mix cornbread with other ingredients as directed on package. Preheat oven to 400°. Grease skillet with nonstick cooking spray and place in oven to preheat for 10 minutes. Spread prepared batter in hot skillet and bake uncovered for 15 to 20 minutes or until light golden brown.

Alternate Cooking Method

To cook it outside on a campfire, use about 26 hot coals and prepare riser in 10" Dutch oven (figure 1). Arrange about ⅓ of the hot coals in a cooking ring and set covered Dutch oven on top to preheat for 5 to 10 minutes. Meanwhile, grease an 8" round metal baking pan with nonstick cooking spray and spread prepared batter in pan. Set pan on riser in hot Dutch oven. Cover pot and place remaining hot coals on lid. Bake for 12 to 18 minutes or until light golden brown and cooked through. Rotate pot and lid once during cooking and adjust the number of coals on top and bottom as needed for even cooking.

COOK IT INSIDE

Griddle

Garlic Toast (from loaf of sliced French bread)

Spread both sides of bread slices with softened butter and sprinkle with garlic powder as desired. Place griddle on stovetop over medium-high heat to preheat. When hot, cook slices for 1 to 3 minutes on each side or until lightly toasted.

Alternate Cooking Method

Cook it outside with a griddle on grate over medium-high heat (hot coals or gas grill).

Old-Fashioned Pork Roast

Serves 8

1 (2 to 3 lb.) boneless pork loin roast
1 tsp. salt
2 tsp. pepper
1 tsp. seasoned salt

1 onion
1 T. olive oil
2½ tsp. minced garlic
1 T. Kitchen Bouquet
2 T. cornstarch

BASIC DIRECTIONS

Cut off excess fat from roast. Season all sides of pork with salt, pepper and seasoned salt. Thinly slice onion. Then cook as directed on next page.

Serve

with mashed potatoes and gravy.

COOK IT INSIDE

10"
w/lid

Stovetop & Oven

Preheat oven to 350°. Meanwhile, place Dutch oven on stovetop over medium-high heat and add oil. When hot, brown roast on all sides. Add onion and garlic; sauté until tender. Mix Kitchen Bouquet with 2 cups water; pour water mixture into Dutch oven and bring to a boil. Cover pot and remove from heat.

Place Dutch oven on lower rack in oven. Cook for 1 hour or until a meat thermometer reaches 145°, turning roast after 30 minutes. Remove roast to a platter and tent with foil to keep warm. Let meat stand 15 minutes before slicing.

To make gravy, set Dutch oven on stovetop over medium-high heat. In a small bowl, mix ½ cup cold water and cornstarch. Whisk cornstarch mixture into drippings in pot; boil and stir until thickened.

COOK IT OUTSIDE

10"
w/lid

Campfire   22 (+) hot coals

Spread the hot coals in a flat layer underneath Dutch oven. Heat oil and brown roast on all sides. Add onion and garlic; sauté until tender. Mix Kitchen Bouquet with 2 cups water. Pour water mixture into Dutch oven and bring to a boil. Cover pot with lid.

Rearrange about ½ of the hot coals to make a cooking ring underneath Dutch oven; place remaining hot coals on lid. Cook about 1 hour or until a meat thermometer reaches 145°, turning roast after 30 minutes. Rotate pot and lid several times during cooking and replenish coals on top and bottom as needed to maintain cooking temperature. Remove roast to a platter and tent with foil to keep warm. Let meat stand 15 minutes before slicing.

To make gravy, transfer several coals from lid to cooking ring underneath Dutch oven. In a small bowl, mix ½ cup cold water and cornstarch. Whisk cornstarch mixture into drippings in pot; boil and stir until thickened.

Chuck Wagon Beef Stew

Serves 5

3 potatoes

2 parsnips

½ (16 oz.) pkg. baby carrots

1 C. frozen corn or mixed vegetables

2 T. flour

1 tsp. paprika

1½ tsp. chili powder, divided

1 tsp. salt

1 lb. cubed beef stew meat

3 T. olive oil

1 C. chopped onion

½ tsp. minced garlic

3 C. beef broth or bouillon

½ tsp. red pepper flakes

Seasoned salt and pepper to taste

Shaved Parmesan cheese, optional

Fresh basil leaves, optional

BASIC DIRECTIONS

Scrub and cube potatoes. Peel and slice parsnips. Place potatoes, parsnips, carrots and corn in a large bowl; reserve for later use. In a gallon-size resealable plastic bag, combine flour, paprika, 1 teaspoon chili powder and salt. Add beef and shake to coat cubes well. Then cook as directed on next page.

Serve

steaming hot in bowls, garnished with Parmesan cheese and basil, if desired.

COOK IT INSIDE

12"
w/lid

Stovetop & Oven

Preheat oven to 275°. Meanwhile, place skillet on stovetop over medium-high heat and add oil. When hot, brown meat on all sides. Add onion; sauté until tender. Stir in garlic and sauté briefly. Reduce heat to medium-low and stir in broth, red pepper flakes, remaining ½ teaspoon chili powder and reserved vegetables. Sprinkle with seasoned salt and pepper. Cover skillet and transfer to oven. Cook about 3 hours or until meat is very tender.

COOK IT OUTSIDE

10"
w/lid

Campfire   16 (+) hot coals

Spread the hot coals in a flat layer underneath Dutch oven and add oil. When hot, brown meat on all sides. Add onion; sauté until tender. Stir in garlic and sauté briefly. Stir in broth, red pepper flakes, remaining ½ teaspoon chili powder and reserved vegetables. Sprinkle with seasoned salt and pepper. Cover pot with lid.

Rearrange about ½ of the hot coals to make a cooking ring underneath Dutch oven; place remaining hot coals on lid. Simmer slowly for 2 to 3 hours, rotating pot and lid several times every hour and replenishing coals on top and bottom as needed to maintain cooking temperature. If necessary, add water to keep liquid at a low simmer.

Alternate Cooking Method

Use a kitchen-style Dutch oven with lid on a grate over medium heat (hot coals or gas grill), simmering until tender. Adjust cooking time as needed.

Variation

Add chopped tomatoes and mushrooms to stew.

Main Dishes

Chicken Pot Pie

Serves 8

1 (9") refrigerated pie crust

1 C. sliced carrot coins

½ C. chopped onion

2 tsp. minced garlic

1 (4 oz.) can sliced mushrooms, drained

1 C. frozen corn, partially thawed

1 C. frozen shredded hash browns, partially thawed

½ C. frozen peas, partially thawed

2 T. olive oil

Salt and pepper to taste

½ tsp. poultry seasoning, optional

3 C. chopped cooked chicken*

1 (10.7 oz.) can cream of potato soup

1 (10.7 oz.) can cream of chicken soup

⅔ C. fat-free half & half

* In place of chicken, you may use leftover cooked turkey or, for convenience, try rotisserie or canned chunk chicken.

BASIC DIRECTIONS

Let pie crust stand at room temperature for 15 minutes (in wrapper). In a medium bowl, combine carrots, onion and garlic; in another bowl, combine mushrooms, corn, hash browns and peas. Then cook as directed on next page.

Serve

in bowls, crust side up.

COOK IT INSIDE

12"

Stovetop & Oven

Preheat oven to 375°. Meanwhile, place skillet on stovetop over medium heat and add oil. When hot, add carrots and onion; sauté until crisp-tender. Stir in garlic and sauté briefly. Add mushrooms, corn, hash browns and peas, tossing to blend. Season with salt, pepper and poultry seasoning as desired. Cook about 2 minutes or until heated through, stirring frequently. Stir in chicken, both soups and half & half; mix gently to blend. Cook until warmed.

Remove skillet from heat. Unroll crust and place over chicken filling to cover, crimping edges as needed. Cut several slits in crust to vent steam. Place skillet on center rack in oven and bake for 40 to 45 minutes or until crust is golden brown and filling is bubbly. Let stand several minutes before serving.

COOK IT OUTSIDE

10"
w/lid

Campfire   24 (+) hot coals

Spread the hot coals in a flat layer underneath Dutch oven. Add oil. When hot, sauté carrots and onion until crisp-tender. Stir in garlic and sauté briefly. Add mushrooms, corn, hash browns and peas, tossing to blend. Season with salt, pepper and poultry seasoning as desired. Cook about 2 minutes or until heated through, stirring frequently. Stir in chicken, both soups and half & half; mix gently to blend. Cook until warmed.

Remove Dutch oven from heat. Unroll crust and place over chicken filling to cover, crimping edges as needed. Cut several slits in crust to vent steam. Cover pot with lid. Rearrange about ⅓ of the hot coals to make a cooking ring underneath Dutch oven; place remaining hot coals on lid. Cook for 40 to 50 minutes or until crust is golden brown and filling is bubbly. Rotate pot and lid several times during cooking and replenish coals on lid toward end of cooking time to promote browning. Let stand several minutes before serving.

Dutch Oven Meatloaf

Serves 16

1 onion
4 lbs. lean ground beef
2 C. bread crumbs
3 eggs, lightly beaten
1 C. milk

1 C. ketchup, divided
2 tsp. salt
½ tsp. pepper
Garlic powder to taste
Vegetable oil

BASIC DIRECTIONS

Finely chop onion and place in a large bowl. Add ground beef, bread crumbs, eggs, milk, ½ cup ketchup, salt, pepper and garlic powder as desired. Mix thoroughly and then cook as directed on next page.

Serve
slices of hot meatloaf with baked or mashed potatoes.

COOK IT INSIDE

Oven

Preheat oven to 350°. Lightly grease bottom of Dutch oven with oil. Spread prepared meatloaf mixture in pot; cover with lid. Place on lower rack in oven and cook for 50 to 60 minutes.

Uncover and spread remaining ½ cup ketchup over meatloaf. Return to oven to bake uncovered for 15 minutes more or until fully cooked (160° internal temperature). Let stand a few minutes before slicing.

COOK IT OUTSIDE

Campfire   24 (+) hot coals

Lightly grease bottom of Dutch oven with vegetable oil. Spread prepared meatloaf mixture in pot and cover with lid.

Arrange about ½ of the hot coals in a cooking ring underneath Dutch oven. Place remaining hot coals on lid. Cook about 40 minutes, rotating pot and lid several times during cooking and replenishing coals on top and bottom as needed to maintain temperature.

Transfer a few hot coals from bottom ring to lid and continue to cook about 20 minutes more. Carefully remove lid and spread remaining ½ cup ketchup over meatloaf; cover again and cook for 15 minutes more or until fully cooked (160° internal temperature). Let stand a few minutes before slicing.

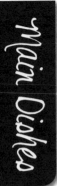

Roasted Chicken & Vegetables

Serves 6

1 (4 to 5 lb.) whole chicken, cut into pieces

⅓ C. flour

1 T. Montreal Chicken Seasoning or chicken rub*

2 T. olive oil

1 onion

3 large carrots, peeled

2 potatoes, peeled

½ butternut squash, peeled

1 zucchini

1 red bell pepper, cored, seeded

2 C. fresh mushrooms

Salt and pepper to taste

2 sprigs fresh rosemary (or 2 tsp. dried)

* In a small bowl, stir together ½ teaspoon each of curry powder, dried sage, dried rosemary, dried coriander, dried thyme and ¼ teaspoon garlic powder.

BASIC DIRECTIONS

Cut off excess fat from chicken; remove skin, if desired. In a shallow bowl, mix flour and Montreal Chicken Seasoning. Coat all sides of chicken pieces in flour mixture; set aside. Cut onion, carrots, potatoes and squash into large chunks. Slice zucchini and bell pepper. Then cook as directed on next page.

Serve

with a large slotted spoon, drizzling juices over chicken and vegetables as desired.

COOK IT INSIDE

Oven

12″ w/lid

Preheat oven to 350°. Meanwhile, place Dutch oven on stovetop over medium-high heat and add oil. When hot, brown chicken pieces on both sides. Remove pot from heat; tuck onion pieces underneath chicken. Arrange carrots, potatoes, zucchini, squash and mushrooms around chicken. Season with salt and pepper; top with rosemary.

Cover Dutch oven and place on lower rack in oven. Cook about 1 hour or until chicken and vegetables are tender. Add bell pepper during last 15 minutes of cooking time. Let stand several minutes before serving.

COOK IT OUTSIDE

Campfire   24 (+) hot coals

12″ w/lid

Spread the hot coals in a flat layer underneath Dutch oven. Heat oil and brown chicken pieces on both sides. Tuck onion pieces underneath chicken. Arrange carrots, potatoes, zucchini, squash and mushrooms around chicken. Season with salt and pepper; top with rosemary. Cover pot with lid.

Rearrange about ⅓ of the hot coals to make a cooking ring underneath Dutch oven; place remaining hot coals on lid. Cook for 50 to 60 minutes or until chicken and vegetables are tender. Add bell pepper during last 15 minutes of cooking time. Rotate pot and lid several times during cooking and replenish coals on top and bottom as needed to maintain cooking temperature. Let stand several minutes before serving.

Barbecued Beef Brisket

Serves 10

1 (3 lb.) beef brisket
2 to 3 onions
½ C. ketchup
½ C. tomato soup
1 T. lemon juice

1 T. brown sugar
1 T. vegetable oil
1 tsp. salt
½ tsp. pepper
Hot sauce to taste, optional

BASIC DIRECTIONS

Trim off excess fat from brisket. Chop onions and set aside. In a small bowl, combine ketchup, soup, lemon juice and brown sugar; mix well and reserve for later use. Then cook as directed on next page.

Serve
slices of hot brisket with remaining sauce in Dutch oven.

COOK IT INSIDE

Stovetop

12" w/lid

Place Dutch oven on stovetop over medium heat and add oil. When hot, brown brisket on all sides. Push meat to one side in pot. Add onions and sauté until tender. Add 2 cups hot water, salt, pepper and hot sauce, if desired. Cover with lid, reduce heat to low and simmer for 1 hour.

Pour reserved ketchup mixture over brisket. Cover and simmer slowly for 1¼ hours more or until meat is tender. Stir occasionally and add more water if necessary. Let brisket stand at least 10 minutes before slicing across the grain.

Alternate Cooking Method

If preferred, transfer Dutch oven from stovetop to a 300° oven for the last 1¼ hours of cooking time.

COOK IT OUTSIDE

Campfire   22 (+) hot coals

12" w/lid

Spread the hot coals in a flat layer underneath Dutch oven and add oil. When hot, brown brisket on all sides. Push brisket to one side in pot. Add onions and sauté until tender. Add 2 cups hot water, salt, pepper and hot sauce, if desired. Cover pot with lid.

Rearrange about ½ of the hot coals to make a cooking ring underneath Dutch oven; place remaining hot coals on lid. Simmer about 1 hour, stirring occasionally and rotating pot and lid several times during cooking. Adjust the number of coals on top and bottom as needed to maintain cooking temperature.

Pour reserved ketchup mixture over brisket. Cover and simmer slowly for 1¼ hours more or until meat is tender. Stir occasionally and add more water if necessary. Rotate pot and lid several times during cooking and replenish coals as needed for even heat. Let brisket stand at least 10 minutes before slicing across the grain.

Hawaiian Chicken

Serves 4

1 C. peach preserves
½ C. barbecue sauce
2 T. soy sauce
½ C. diced onion
1 green bell pepper, cored, seeded
⅓ C. flour
½ tsp. paprika

½ tsp. salt
Dash of pepper
2 T. vegetable oil
4 boneless, skinless chicken breast halves
1 (8 oz.) can sliced water chestnuts, drained
Hot cooked rice

BASIC DIRECTIONS

In a medium bowl, stir together peach preserves, barbecue sauce, soy sauce and onion; reserve sauce for later use. Slice bell pepper into strips. In a shallow bowl, combine flour, paprika, salt and pepper; mix well. Coat both sides of chicken breast halves in flour mixture. Then cook as directed on next page.

Serve
with cooked rice.

COOK IT INSIDE

12" w/lid

Stovetop & Oven

Preheat oven to 350°. Meanwhile, place skillet on stovetop over medium-high heat and add oil. When hot, brown chicken pieces on each side for 3 minutes. Remove skillet from heat and pour off excess oil. Pour reserved barbecue sauce mixture over chicken.

Cover skillet and place on center rack in oven to cook for 35 minutes. Remove lid and stir in bell pepper and water chestnuts. Cover and return to oven to cook about 15 minutes more or until tender.

COOK IT OUTSIDE

12" w/lid

Campfire | 26 (+) hot coals

Spread the hot coals in a flat layer underneath Dutch oven. Pour oil into pot. When hot, brown chicken pieces on each side for 3 minutes. Remove pot from coals and pour off excess oil. Pour reserved barbeque sauce mixture over chicken and cover pot with lid.

Rearrange about ⅓ of the hot coals to make a cooking ring underneath Dutch oven; place remaining hot coals on lid. Cook for 30 to 40 minutes, rotating pot and lid twice during cooking and replenishing coals on top and bottom as needed to maintain cooking temperature. Remove lid and stir in bell pepper and water chestnuts. Cover and cook about 15 minutes more or until tender.

Alternate Cooking Method

Use a kitchen-style Dutch oven with lid and cook on a grate over medium heat (hot coals or grill).

Pork Chop Bake

Serves 4

¼ C. lite soy sauce
3 T. honey
1 tsp. chili powder
1 tsp. curry powder
Pepper to taste
5 bacon strips

4 pork chops (1" thick)
⅔ C. chopped onion
½ tsp. minced garlic
Hot cooked brown rice or noodles

BASIC DIRECTIONS

In a small bowl, combine soy sauce, honey, chili powder, curry powder and pepper; mix well and reserve for later use. Cut bacon into small pieces. Then cook as directed on next page.

Serve
with cooked rice or noodles.

COOK IT INSIDE

12" w/lid

Stovetop & Oven

Preheat oven to 350°. Meanwhile, place skillet on stovetop over medium heat and brown pork chops for 5 to 6 minutes on each side. Remove chops to a platter and tent with foil to keep warm. Pour off any accumulated grease.

Lightly brown bacon in skillet; then add onion and sauté over medium heat for 5 minutes. Add garlic and sauté briefly. Pour off excess grease and stir in reserved soy sauce mixture. Place pork chops back in skillet and turn to coat with sauce. Cover skillet and place on center rack in oven to bake for 20 to 25 minutes or until chops are cooked through and tender. Let cooked chops stand at least 3 minutes before serving.

COOK IT OUTSIDE

12" w/lid

Campfire — about 26 hot coals

Spread the hot coals in a flat layer underneath Dutch oven. Add pork chops and brown meat for 5 to 6 minutes on each side. Remove chops to a platter and tent with foil to keep warm. Pour off any accumulated grease.

Lightly brown bacon in Dutch oven; then add onion and sauté for 5 minutes. Add garlic and sauté briefly. Pour off excess grease and stir in reserved soy sauce mixture.

Rearrange about ⅓ of the hot coals to make a cooking ring underneath Dutch oven. Place pork chops back in pot and turn to coat with sauce. Cover Dutch oven and place remaining hot coals on lid. Cook for 20 to 30 minutes or until chops are cooked through and tender. Rotate pot and lid twice during cooking time and adjust the number of coals on top and bottom as needed for even cooking. Let cooked chops stand at least 3 minutes before serving.

Simple Round Steak

Serves 8

1½ to 2 lbs. round steak
1 onion
1 green bell pepper, cored, seeded
1 (12 oz.) can cola

¾ C. ketchup
2 T. olive oil
Salt and pepper to taste
Hot cooked noodles

BASIC DIRECTIONS

Cut round steak into eight equal strips. Slice onion and bell pepper. In a medium bowl, whisk together cola and ketchup. Then cook as directed on next page.

Serve
with sauce and cooked noodles.

COOK IT INSIDE

12" w/lid

Stovetop & Oven

Preheat oven to 325°. Meanwhile, place skillet on stovetop over medium heat and add oil. When hot, brown steak pieces on both sides. Add onion and sauté until tender. Remove pan from heat and remove meat and onion from skillet; pour off oil.

Return meat and onion to skillet and add bell pepper. Pour prepared cola mixture over meat; season with salt and pepper as desired. Cover with lid and place skillet on center rack in oven to cook about 1 hour or until meat is tender and sauce thickens.

COOK IT OUTSIDE

12" w/lid

Campfire   24 (+) hot coals

Spread the hot coals in a flat layer underneath Dutch oven and add oil. When hot, brown steak pieces on both sides. Add onion and sauté until tender. Remove pot from heat and remove meat and onion from pot; pour off oil.

Return meat and onion to pot and add bell pepper. Pour prepared cola mixture over meat; season with salt and pepper as desired. Cover pot with lid.

Rearrange about ⅓ of the hot coals to make a cooking ring underneath Dutch oven; place remaining hot coals on lid. Cook about 1 hour or until meat is tender and sauce thickens. Rotate pot and lid several times during cooking and replenish coals on top and bottom as needed to maintain cooking temperature.

Variation

Add ¼ cup teriyaki sauce and 1 teaspoon garlic powder while browning round steak. Do not drain. Add ¼ cup chopped jalapeño peppers and 1 teaspoon red pepper flakes before cooking.

Cheesy Potatoes & Ham

Serves 5

1½ C. diced ham
3 C. diced raw potatoes
¼ C. butter
1 C. chopped onion
3 T. flour
2 C. milk

1 T. parsley flakes
1 tsp. dried minced garlic
Salt and pepper to taste
½ C. shredded Cheddar cheese
3 T. Italian bread crumbs

BASIC DIRECTIONS

In a medium bowl, combine ham and potatoes. Then cook as directed on next page.

Serve

promptly. Add a side salad or raw vegetables and dip to complete the meal.

COOK IT INSIDE

10"

Stovetop & Oven

Preheat oven to 400°. Meanwhile, place Dutch oven on stovetop over medium heat and melt butter. Add onion and sauté until tender. Stir in flour until bubbly and light brown. Gradually whisk in milk and cook until thickened. Stir in parsley and garlic.

Remove pot from heat and add ham and potato mixture to sauce, stirring gently to coat. Season with salt and pepper. Spread mixture in pot and sprinkle with cheese and bread crumbs. Place pot on center rack in oven and bake uncovered for 20 minutes or until heated through and lightly browned.

COOK IT OUTSIDE

10"
w/lid

Campfire · about 26 hot coals

Spread ½ the hot coals in a flat layer underneath Dutch oven. Melt butter; add onion and sauté until tender. Stir in flour until bubbly and light brown. Gradually whisk in milk and cook until thickened. Stir in parsley and garlic.

Remove pot from heat and add ham and potato mixture to sauce, stirring gently to coat. Season with salt and pepper. Spread mixture evenly in pot and sprinkle with cheese and bread crumbs. Cover pot with lid.

Rearrange the hot coals to make a cooking ring that just fits underneath Dutch oven; place remaining hot coals on lid. Cook about 20 minutes or until heated through and lightly browned. Rotate pot and lid halfway through cooking time and adjust the number of coals on top and bottom as needed for even cooking.

Pizza Casserole

Serves 12

3 C. uncooked macaroni, bow tie pasta or spaghetti

½ tsp. olive oil

2 lbs. ground sausage

1 C. finely chopped onion

1 tsp. minced garlic

1 C. sliced fresh mushrooms

2 (14 oz.) jars pizza sauce

1 (6 oz.) can tomato paste

1½ tsp. dried oregano

3 C. shredded mozzarella cheese

¾ C. grated Parmesan cheese

1 (3 oz.) pkg. sliced pepperoni

BASIC DIRECTIONS

In a large pot* of lightly salted boiling water, cook macaroni until tender. Drain and toss macaroni with oil; set aside. (This can be done ahead of time, if desired.) Finish cooking as directed on next page.

* You may use a Dutch oven pot over medium-high heat on stovetop or over a spread of hot coals on a campfire or gas grill.

Serve

with a salad and garlic toast (see page 55 for grilling toast).

COOK IT INSIDE

Stovetop & Oven

Preheat oven to 350°. Place Dutch oven on stovetop over medium-high heat and add sausage, onion and garlic. Cook and stir until meat is crumbly and lightly browned and onion is tender; drain. Stir in mushrooms, pizza sauce, tomato paste and oregano; reduce heat to low and simmer sauce mixture for 15 minutes, stirring frequently.

Add cooked pasta and stir to combine. Remove from heat and top with mozzarella and Parmesan cheeses. Arrange pepperoni over top. Place Dutch oven on lower rack in oven and bake uncovered for 25 to 30 minutes or until heated through. Let cool 10 to 15 minutes before serving.

COOK IT OUTSIDE

Campfire or Grill | about 24 hot coals

Spread the hot coals in a flat layer underneath Dutch oven. Combine sausage, onion and garlic in pot. Cook and stir until meat is crumbly and lightly browned and onion is tender; drain. Stir in mushrooms, pizza sauce, tomato paste and oregano.

To reduce heat, push about ⅔ of the coals to one side of Dutch oven and simmer the sauce mixture over remaining coals for 15 minutes, stirring frequently. Stir in cooked pasta until well combined. Top with mozzarella and Parmesan cheeses; arrange pepperoni over top. Cover pot with lid.

Rearrange the hot coals under Dutch oven to make a cooking ring and place remaining hot coals on lid. Cook for 20 to 30 minutes or until heated through. Rotate pot and lid twice during cooking and adjust the number of coals on top and bottom as needed for even cooking. Let cool 10 to 15 minutes before serving

Calico Chili

Serves 6

2 bell peppers (assortment of green, yellow, red, orange), cored, seeded

1 lb. lean ground beef

¾ C. chopped onion

1 tsp. minced garlic

1 (16 oz.) can chili beans, undrained

1 (16 oz.) can Northern beans, drained, rinsed

1 (14.5 oz.) can diced tomatoes, undrained

1¼ C. tomato juice or V-8 juice

1⅓ C. frozen or canned whole kernel corn, drained

1 (1 oz.) env. ranch salad dressing mix

Corn chips, optional

Shredded Cheddar cheese, optional

BASIC DIRECTIONS

Chop bell peppers to measure 1¾ cups. Then proceed as directed on next page.

Serve

in bowls garnished with a few corn chips and cheese, if desired. Bake cornbread (recipes on pages 38 and 40), biscuits (recipe on page 32) or sourdough bread (recipe on page 46) to serve with chili.

COOK IT INSIDE

Stovetop

Place Dutch oven on stovetop over medium-high heat and add ground beef and onion. Cook and stir until meat is crumbly and lightly browned and onion is tender; drain.

Add garlic and bell peppers; cook for 3 minutes to soften. Stir in 1 cup water, chili beans, Northern beans, tomatoes, tomato juice, corn and dressing mix until well combined. Bring to a simmer, stirring frequently. Reduce heat to low, cover and simmer slowly for 20 to 30 minutes, stirring occasionally, until flavors are blended.

COOK IT OUTSIDE

Campfire or Grill   about 24 hot coals

Spread the hot coals in a flat layer underneath Dutch oven. Add ground beef and onion to pot. Cook and stir until meat is crumbly and lightly browned and onion is tender; drain. Add garlic and bell peppers; cook for 3 minutes to soften. Stir in 1 cup water, chili beans, Northern beans, tomatoes, tomato juice, corn and dressing mix until well combined. Bring to a simmer, stirring frequently. Cover pot with lid.

Rearrange about ½ of the hot coals to make a cooking ring underneath Dutch oven; place remaining hot coals on lid. Simmer slowly for 20 to 30 minutes, stirring occasionally, until flavors are blended. Rotate pot and lid once during cooking time and adjust the number of coals on top and bottom as needed for even cooking.

Swiss Crabmeat Bake

Serves 6

1½ C. flour, divided

1 tsp. salt, divided

2 tsp. baking powder

1¼ C. shredded Swiss cheese, divided

2 T. plus ½ C. butter, divided

½ C. chopped green bell pepper

½ C. chopped onion

1 tsp. dry mustard

1½ C. milk, divided

1 (8 oz.) pkg. imitation crabmeat

½ C. chopped Roma tomatoes

2 tsp. Worcestershire sauce

BASIC DIRECTIONS

In a medium bowl, combine 1 cup flour, ½ teaspoon salt and baking powder. Stir in ¼ cup Swiss cheese. With a pastry blender or two knives, cut in 2 tablespoons butter until mixture is crumbly; reserve for later use. Then proceed as directed on next page.

Serve promptly.

COOK IT INSIDE

10"

Preheat oven to 400°. Meanwhile, place skillet on stovetop over medium heat and melt remaining ½ cup butter. Add bell pepper and onion; sauté until tender. Gradually blend in remaining ½ cup flour, dry mustard, 1 cup milk and remaining 1 cup cheese. Reduce heat to low and cook until cheese melts, stirring constantly. Add crabmeat, tomatoes and Worcestershire sauce; cook and stir until mixture is hot. Spread evenly in skillet and remove from heat.

To reserved flour mixture, add remaining ½ cup milk and stir until dough forms. Drop dough by small spoonfuls over hot crab mixture, like a cobbler topping. Transfer skillet to center rack in oven and bake uncovered about 25 minutes or until topping is golden brown and no longer doughy. Let cool slightly before serving.

COOK IT OUTSIDE

10" w/lid

Campfire | about 24 hot coals

Arrange about ½ of the hot coals in a cooking ring underneath Dutch oven. Melt butter in pot. Add bell pepper and onion; sauté until tender. Blend in remaining ½ cup flour, dry mustard, 1 cup milk and remaining 1 cup cheese. Remove about four hot coals from cooking ring to reduce heat; cook mixture until cheese melts, stirring constantly. Add crabmeat, tomatoes and Worcestershire sauce; cook and stir until mixture is hot.

To reserved flour mixture, add remaining ½ cup milk and stir until dough forms. Drop dough by small spoonfuls over hot crab mixture, like a cobbler topping. Cover pot and place remaining hot coals on lid. Cook for 20 to 30 minutes or until topping is golden brown and no longer doughy. Rotate pot and lid twice during cooking and adjust the number of coals on top and bottom as needed for even cooking. Let cool slightly before serving.

Deep-Dish Pizza

Serves 4

1¼ tsp. active dry yeast
2 tsp. sugar
1 tsp. salt
¼ tsp. garlic powder
1 T. olive oil
1½ to 2 C. bread flour
½ C. prepared pizza sauce

Toppings such as sliced pepperoni, browned sausage or ground beef, sliced red onion, sliced mushrooms, chopped bell pepper, green or black olives, anchovies

1 to 1½ C. shredded mozzarella cheese

2 T. grated Parmesan cheese

Freshly ground pepper

Chopped fresh basil, optional

BASIC DIRECTIONS

In a medium bowl, combine yeast, sugar and ½ cup very warm water; stir to dissolve and let stand until foamy, about 10 minutes. Stir in salt, garlic powder, oil and just enough flour to make a dough that pulls away from the side of the bowl. Turn dough out on a lightly floured surface and knead for 5 minutes; cover and let rest 30 to 60 minutes. Then proceed as directed on next page.

Serve
promptly.

COOK IT INSIDE

10"

Stovetop & Oven

Preheat oven to 450°. Lightly grease skillet with nonstick cooking spray. Roll out dough in a circle about 1" larger on all sides than skillet; place dough in pan.* Pinch edges to form a rim. Spread sauce over crust. Sprinkle with desired toppings, finishing with mozzarella and Parmesan cheeses. Sprinkle with pepper.

Place skillet on stovetop over high heat for 3 minutes to begin cooking bottom of crust. Transfer skillet to lower rack in oven and bake for 15 to 20 minutes or until crust is golden brown and cheese is melted. Let cool slightly before sliding pizza out of skillet; sprinkle with fresh basil, if desired. Slice to serve.

* For thinner crust, use a 12" skillet and shorten baking time slightly.

COOK IT OUTSIDE

12"
w/lid

Campfire | about 27 hot coals

Lightly grease a 9" to 10" deep metal pie plate with nonstick cooking spray. Roll out dough in a circle about 1" larger on all sides than plate.* Press dough into plate and up sides, pinching edges to form a rim. Spread sauce over crust. Sprinkle with desired toppings, finishing with mozzarella and Parmesan cheeses. Sprinkle with pepper. Prepare riser in dutch oven (figure 1 on page 54). Set pie plate on riser and cover pot with lid.

Arrange about ⅓ of the hot coals in a cooking ring underneath Dutch oven. Place remaining hot coals on lid. Cook for 15 to 25 minutes or until crust is golden brown and cheese is melted. Rotate pot and lid twice during cooking and adjust the number of coals on top and bottom as needed for even cooking. Let cool slightly before removing pie plate from Dutch oven. Sprinkle with fresh basil, if desired. Slice to serve.

* For thinner crust, divide dough in half and make two pizzas. Shorten cooking time slightly.

Dutch Oven Party Potatoes

Serves 12

1 (10.7 oz.) can cream of chicken soup

1 (10.7 oz.) can cream of mushroom soup

2 C. sour cream

1½ C. shredded Cheddar cheese

¼ tsp. pepper

1 (30 oz.) bag frozen shredded or cubed hash browns,* partially thawed

⅓ C. chopped green onions

2 C. crushed corn flakes cereal

¼ C. butter, melted

Sliced green onions, optional

* In place of frozen hash browns, peel 12 large potatoes; boil in lightly salted water for 30 minutes or until almost tender. Cool completely. Grate or dice into a large bowl and proceed as directed.

BASIC DIRECTIONS

In a large bowl, combine both cans of soup, sour cream, cheese and pepper; stir to blend. Add hash browns and chopped green onions; mix well. Then proceed as directed on next page.

Serve

promptly alongside any main dish. Garnish with sliced green onions, if desired.

COOK IT INSIDE

Oven

12"

Preheat oven to 350°. Lightly grease Dutch oven with nonstick cooking spray. Spoon prepared potato mixture into pot and spread evenly.

In a small bowl, stir together cereal and melted butter; sprinkle evenly over potato mixture. Place pot on center rack in oven and bake uncovered about 40 minutes or until hot and bubbly. Let stand 5 minutes before serving.

COOK IT OUTSIDE

Campfire | about 24 hot coals

12" w/lid

Lightly grease Dutch oven with nonstick cooking spray. Spoon prepared potato mixture into pot and spread evenly.

In a small bowl, stir together cereal and melted butter; sprinkle evenly over potato mixture. Cover pot with lid.

Arrange about ½ of the hot coals in a cooking ring underneath Dutch oven. Place remaining hot coals on lid. Cook for 25 to 30 minutes or until hot and bubbly. Rotate pot and lid twice during cooking and adjust the number of coals on top and bottom as needed for even cooking. Let stand 5 minutes before serving.

Alternate Cooking Method

Use a kitchen-style Dutch oven with lid and cook on a grate over medium heat (hot coals or gas heat). Allow extra cooking time.

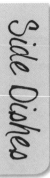
Potatoes au Gratin

Serves 8

3 lbs. russet potatoes, peeled

1¼ C. shredded Cheddar cheese

1¼ C. shredded Monterey Jack cheese

½ C. grated Parmesan cheese

2 tsp. cornstarch

¾ C. heavy cream

½ C. low-sodium chicken broth

½ tsp. garlic powder, optional

Salt and pepper to taste

BASIC DIRECTIONS

With a sharp knife or mandolin, thinly slice potatoes (about ⅛" thickness) and place in a large bowl. In another large bowl, combine Cheddar, Monterey Jack and Parmesan cheeses with cornstarch and toss until evenly coated.

In a large measuring cup, combine cream, broth and garlic powder, if desired; stir to blend and reserve for later use. Then proceed as directed on next page.

Serve family style with a large spoon.

COOK IT INSIDE

Oven

Preheat oven to 350°. Lightly grease Dutch oven with nonstick cooking spray. Layer half the sliced potatoes in pot. Sprinkle potatoes with 1½ cups cheese mixture and season lightly with salt and pepper. Layer remaining potatoes over cheese and sprinkle with salt and pepper. Pour reserved cream mixture evenly over potatoes and top with remaining cheese mixture.

Cover pot with lid and place on center rack in oven to bake about 1 hour. Remove lid and bake uncovered for 15 to 20 minutes more or until golden brown and tender. Let cool about 10 minutes before serving.

COOK IT OUTSIDE

Campfire 26 (+) hot coals

Lightly grease Dutch oven with nonstick cooking spray. Layer half the sliced potatoes in pot. Sprinkle potatoes with 1½ cups cheese mixture and season lightly with salt and pepper. Layer remaining potatoes over cheese and sprinkle with salt and pepper. Pour reserved cream mixture evenly over potatoes and top with remaining cheese mixture. Cover pot with lid.

Arrange about ⅓ of the hot coals in a cooking ring underneath Dutch oven. Place remaining hot coals on lid. Cook for 1 hour 20 minutes or until golden brown and tender. Rotate pot and lid every 15 minutes during cooking and replenish coals on top and bottom as needed to maintain cooking temperature. Let cool about 10 minutes before serving.

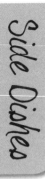

Side Dishes

Cheesy Baked Corn

Serves 8

1 (15.2 oz.) can
cream-style corn

1 (15.2 oz.) can whole kernel
corn, drained

½ C. cornmeal

1 tsp. garlic salt

½ C. grated Parmesan cheese

1½ C. shredded
Cheddar cheese

1 tsp. baking powder

¼ to ½ C. vegetable oil

2 eggs, lightly beaten

½ tsp. onion powder,
optional

BASIC DIRECTIONS

In a large bowl, combine cream-style corn, whole kernel corn, cornmeal, garlic salt, Parmesan cheese, Cheddar cheese, baking powder and oil; mix well. Add eggs and stir to blend. Stir in onion powder, if desired. Then bake as directed on next page.

Serve
promptly.

COOK IT INSIDE

Oven

Preheat oven to 350°. Grease bottom and sides of Dutch oven with nonstick cooking spray. Pour prepared corn mixture into pot and place on center rack in oven. Bake uncovered for 40 to 45 minutes or until lightly browned and heated through.

COOK IT OUTSIDE

Campfire   22 (+) hot coals

Grease bottom and sides of Dutch oven with nonstick cooking spray. Pour prepared corn mixture into pot and cover with lid.

Arrange about ⅓ of the hot coals in a cooking ring underneath Dutch oven. Place remaining hot coals on lid. Cook for 35 to 45 minutes, rotating pot and lid several times during cooking and replenishing coals on top and bottom as needed to maintain temperature.

Variation

Add one 4-ounce can chopped green chiles for a little kick.

Tip

After eating, remove leftovers from cast iron cookware for storage or food may pick up a metallic taste.

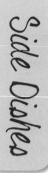
Vegetable & Stuffing Bake

Serves 8

32 oz. assorted frozen
vegetables, any
combination, thawed
(such as cauliflower, corn,
broccoli, carrots, green
beans or snow peas)

1 (6 oz.) pkg. cornbread
stuffing mix, divided

1 T. vegetable oil
¾ C. chopped onion
1 tsp. minced garlic
1 (10.7 oz.) can cream of
celery soup
1 C. Cheez Whiz
2 T. butter, melted, optional

BASIC DIRECTIONS

In a large bowl, combine vegetables and 1 cup dry stuffing mix;
toss to combine and reserve for later use. Then proceed as directed on
next page.

Serve
family style with a large spoon while hot.

COOK IT INSIDE

Stovetop & Oven

Preheat oven to 350°. Meanwhile, place Dutch oven on stovetop over medium heat and add oil. When hot, sauté onion until tender. Add garlic and sauté briefly. Stir in soup and Cheez Whiz until blended; cook until heated through, stirring frequently.

Remove pot from heat and add reserved stuffing mixture; stir well to combine. Spread mixture in pot and sprinkle remaining dry stuffing mix over top. Drizzle with melted butter, if desired. Transfer pot to center rack in oven and bake uncovered for 30 to 35 minutes or until vegetables are tender and mixture is bubbly. Let stand several minutes before serving.

COOK IT OUTSIDE

Campfire | about 22 hot coals

Spread most of the hot coals in a flat layer underneath Dutch oven. Pour oil into pot. When hot, sauté onion until tender. Add garlic and sauté briefly. Stir in soup and Cheez whiz until blended; cook just until heated through, stirring frequently.

Remove pot from heat and add reserved stuffing mixture; stir well to combine. Spread mixture in pot and sprinkle remaining dry stuffing mix over top. Drizzle with melted butter, if desired. Cover with lid.

Arrange about ⅓ of the hot coals in a cooking ring underneath Dutch oven. Place remaining hot coals on lid. Cook for 25 to 35 minutes or until vegetables are tender and mixture is bubbly. Rotate pot and lid twice during cooking and adjust the number of coals on top and bottom as needed for even cooking. Let stand several minutes before serving.

Alternate Cooking Method

Use a kitchen-style Dutch oven with lid and cook on a grate over medium heat (hot coals or gas grill). Allow extra cooking time.

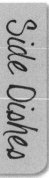

Green Beans & Red Potatoes

Serves 8

6 bacon strips

3 lbs. fresh green beans

12 small red potatoes

1 onion

2¼ C. chicken broth, divided

2 tsp. salt

½ tsp. pepper

½ tsp. garlic powder

¼ to ½ C. butter, sliced

BASIC DIRECTIONS

Cut bacon strips into small pieces. Rinse green beans and remove ends; cut in half. Scrub potatoes and slice onion; set aside. Then proceed as directed on next page.

Serve warm.

COOK IT INSIDE

12" w/lid

Stovetop

Place Dutch oven on stovetop over medium heat and add bacon; cook and stir until crisp. Add green beans to pot, stirring to coat. Stir in 2 cups broth, salt, pepper and garlic powder. Cover with lid and reduce heat to medium-low; cook for 20 to 30 minutes or until green beans are partially cooked.

Add potatoes and onion to pot and stir in remaining ¼ cup broth as needed. Cover and simmer slowly until potatoes are tender, about 30 minutes, checking often to keep some liquid in pot. When potatoes are tender, reduce heat to low and stir in butter as desired. When melted, cover pot and remove from heat to stand for 15 minutes or until green beans are wilted.

COOK IT OUTSIDE

12" w/lid

Campfire   26 (+) hot coals

Spread the hot coals in a flat layer underneath Dutch oven. Place bacon in pot and cook until crisp. Add green beans, stirring to coat. Stir in 2 cups broth, salt, pepper and garlic powder. When hot, cover with lid and remove pot from heat.

Rearrange about ½ of the hot coals to make a cooking ring underneath Dutch oven; place remaining hot coals on lid. Cook for 20 to 30 minutes or until beans are partially cooked, rotating pot and lid twice.

Add potatoes and onion; stir in remaining ¼ cup broth as needed. Cover and simmer slowly until potatoes are tender, about 30 minutes. Rotate pot and lid two more times during cooking and check to keep some liquid in pot. Replenish coals on top and bottom as needed to maintain cooking temperature. When potatoes are tender, remove Dutch oven from heat and stir in butter as desired. Cover and let stand for 15 minutes or until green beans are wilted.

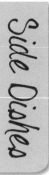
Spanish Rice

Serves 8

1 green bell pepper, cored, seeded

1 red bell pepper, cored, seeded

2 celery ribs

2 onions

3 T. vegetable oil

2 C. uncooked white rice

2 tsp. cumin seeds, crushed

1 tsp. salt

½ tsp. pepper

¼ tsp. garlic powder

6 C. chicken broth (or water)

1 (8 oz.) can tomato sauce

BASIC DIRECTIONS

Finely chop both bell peppers, celery and onions. Then proceed as directed on next page.

Serve
hot alongside meat, poultry or Mexican dishes.

COOK IT INSIDE

Stovetop

Place Dutch oven on stovetop over medium-high heat and add oil. When hot, add bell peppers, celery, onions, rice, cumin, salt, pepper and garlic powder. Sauté until rice is translucent and just beginning to brown, stirring frequently.

Stir in broth and tomato sauce until well combined. Bring mixture to a full boil. Reduce heat to medium-low, cover with lid and simmer slowly for 25 minutes or until rice is tender and liquid has been absorbed.

COOK-IT-OUTSIDE

Campfire — about 26 hot coals

Spread the hot coals in a flat layer underneath Dutch oven. Heat oil and add bell peppers, celery, onion, rice, cumin, salt, pepper and garlic powder. Sauté until rice is translucent and just beginning to brown, stirring frequently.

Stir in broth and tomato sauce until well combined. Bring mixture to a full boil and cover pot. Rearrange ½ of the hot coals to make a cooking ring underneath Dutch oven. Transfer remaining hot coals to lid. Simmer slowly for 20 to 25 minutes or until rice is tender and liquid has been absorbed. Rotate pot and lid twice during cooking and adjust the number of coals on top and bottom as needed for even cooking.

Alternate Cooking Method

Use a kitchen-style Dutch oven with lid and cook on a grate over medium heat (hot coals or gas grill). Stir frequently and adjust cooking time as needed.

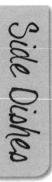

Glazed Autumn Vegetables

Serves 8

3 parsnips
5 large carrots
1 butternut squash
2 sweet potatoes
½ C. butter

¾ C. brown sugar
¼ C. maple syrup
2 tsp. ground cinnamon
1½ tsp. ground nutmeg
Salt and pepper to taste

BASIC DIRECTIONS

Peel parsnips, carrots, squash and sweet potatoes. Cut all vegetables into 1" chunks. Then cook as directed on next page.

Serve
promptly, spooning extra glaze over vegetables.

COOK IT INSIDE

Stovetop & Oven

Preheat oven to 325°. Meanwhile, place Dutch oven on stovetop over medium heat and melt butter. Stir in brown sugar, syrup, cinnamon and nutmeg until well blended. Add vegetables and toss to coat. Season with salt and pepper as desired.

Cover Dutch oven and place on center rack in oven to cook about 35 minutes. Remove lid, stir once and bake uncovered for 15 to 20 minutes more or until vegetables are tender and glazed.

Alternate Cooking Method

Recipe may be cut in half and cooked in a 10" skillet with lid as directed.

COOK IT OUTSIDE

Campfire about 20 hot coals

Arrange about ½ of the hot coals in a cooking ring underneath Dutch oven. Melt butter in pot. Stir in brown sugar, syrup, cinnamon and nutmeg until well blended. Add vegetables and toss to coat. Season with salt and pepper as desired.

Cover pot and place remaining hot coals on lid. Cook for 30 to 35 minutes, rotating pot and lid twice during cooking. Adjust the number of coals on top and bottom as needed for even cooking.

Remove lid and stir once. Cook uncovered about 20 minutes more or until vegetables are tender and glazed, rotating pot and stirring again during cooking.

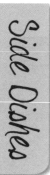

Spicy Baked Beans

Serves 6

1 onion

1 green or yellow bell pepper, cored, seeded

1 (28 oz.) can plain pork and beans

1 T. chili powder

3 T. Worcestershire sauce

2 T. apple cider vinegar

½ C. brown sugar

½ C. ketchup

1 tsp. garlic powder

Salt to taste

Dash of cayenne pepper, optional

BASIC DIRECTIONS

Dice onion and bell pepper. Drain pork and beans. Then cook as directed on next page.

Serve
warm with sandwiches or grilled meats.

COOK IT INSIDE

Oven

10" w/lid

Preheat oven to 350°. Place onion and bell pepper in Dutch oven. Add beans, chili powder, Worcestershire sauce, vinegar, brown sugar, ketchup and garlic powder; stir until blended. Season with salt and cayenne pepper, if desired.

Cover with lid and place on center rack in oven. Bake for 1 hour, uncovering pot during the last 20 to 30 minutes to thicken sauce.

COOK IT OUTSIDE

Campfire · 21 (+) hot coals

10" w/lid

Place onion and bell pepper in Dutch oven. Add beans, chili powder, Worcestershire sauce, vinegar, brown sugar, ketchup and garlic powder; stir until blended. Season with salt and cayenne pepper, if desired. Cover pot with lid.

Arrange about ⅓ of the hot coals in a cooking ring underneath Dutch oven. Place remaining hot coals on lid. Cook for 1 hour, rotating pot and lid several times during cooking and replenishing hot coals on top and bottom as needed to maintain cooking temperature. During the last 20 minutes of cooking, carefully remove lid. Transfer several hot coals from lid to cooking ring underneath pot to maintain heat and promote thickening. Stir as needed.

Alternate Cooking Method

Use a kitchen-style Dutch oven with lid and cook on a grate over medium heat (hot coals or gas grill). Stir often and adjust cooking time as needed.

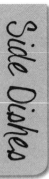

Side Dishes

Roasted Herbed Vegetables

Serves 6

¼ C. olive oil
¾ tsp. garlic salt
¾ tsp. dried oregano
½ tsp. dried thyme
¼ tsp. pepper

½ tsp. sugar
2 (12 oz.) pkgs. frozen vegetables (such as broccoli, cauliflower and carrots), partially thawed

BASIC DIRECTIONS

In a small bowl, combine oil, garlic salt, oregano, thyme, pepper and sugar; stir to blend. Then cook as directed on next page.

Serve promptly.

COOK IT INSIDE

14"

Oven

Preheat oven to 425°. Place vegetables in Dutch oven. Drizzle with oil mixture and toss to coat evenly. Spread vegetables in a single layer in pot and place on center rack in oven. Roast uncovered for 20 to 25 minutes or until tender, stirring occasionally.

COOK IT OUTSIDE

**14"
w/lid**

Campfire | **about 36 hot coals**

Place vegetables in Dutch oven. Drizzle with oil mixture and toss to coat evenly. Spread vegetables in a single layer in pot and cover pot.

Arrange ⅓ to ½ of the hot coals in a cooking ring underneath Dutch oven. Place remaining hot coals on lid. Cook for 15 to 25 minutes, stirring occasionally. Rotate pot and lid at least once during cooking and adjust the number of coals on top and bottom as needed for even cooking.

Tip

In general, if you use a Dutch oven or skillet larger or smaller than the size listed in a recipe, adjust the cooking time accordingly, allowing extra time for thicker mixtures or batters. To cook this recipe in a 10" or 12" Dutch oven, cut ingredients in half.

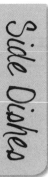

Zucchini-Tomato Bake

Serves 8

1 onion
2 Roma tomatoes
3 zucchini
2 eggs
½ C. half & half
¼ C. shredded
    Cheddar cheese

1 T. olive oil
1½ tsp. minced garlic
1 tsp. ground thyme
1 tsp. salt
2 T. flour
¼ C. grated Parmesan &
    Romano cheese blend

BASIC DIRECTIONS

Chop onion and tomatoes. Slice each zucchini into ½"-thick rounds; cut rounds in half.

In a small bowl, whisk together eggs and half & half. Stir in Cheddar cheese and set aside. Then cook as directed on next page.

Serve
promptly.

COOK IT INSIDE

Stovetop & Oven

10"

Preheat oven to 350°. Meanwhile, place Dutch oven on stovetop over medium-high heat. Add oil; when hot, sauté onion and tomatoes until onion is tender. Add garlic and cook briefly. Stir in zucchini, thyme, salt and flour; cook until zucchini is tender.

Spread vegetable mixture in pot. Pour set-aside egg mixture over vegetables and sprinkle with Parmesan & Romano cheese blend. Bake uncovered for 30 to 35 minutes or until puffed and lightly browned on top.

COOK IT OUTSIDE

Campfire | about 22 hot coals

10" w/lid

Spread most of the hot coals in a flat layer underneath Dutch oven. Heat oil in pot and add onion and tomatoes; sauté until onion is tender. Add garlic and cook briefly. Stir in zucchini, thyme, salt and flour and cook until zucchini is tender.

Spread vegetable mixture in pot. Pour set-aside egg mixture over vegetables and sprinkle with Parmesan & Romano cheese blend. Cover pot with lid.

Arrange about 1/3 of the hot coals in a cooking ring underneath Dutch oven; place remaining hot coals on lid. Cook for 25 to 35 minutes or until puffed and lightly browned on top. Rotate pot and lid twice during cooking and adjust the number of coals on top and bottom for even cooking.

Cinnamon-Pecan Cake

Serves 12

2¼ C. flour
½ tsp. salt
1 T. plus ½ tsp. ground cinnamon, divided
1 C. sugar, divided
1 C. brown sugar
1 tsp. baking powder

1 C. milk
½ C. vegetable oil
1 egg, beaten
½ C. chopped pecans
Whipped topping or vanilla or cinnamon ice cream, optional

BASIC DIRECTIONS

In a medium bowl, stir together flour, salt, 1 tablespoon cinnamon, ¾ cup sugar, brown sugar and baking powder. In a large measuring cup, whisk together milk, oil and egg. Add milk mixture to dry ingredients and stir until batter is smooth.

In a small bowl, mix remaining ½ teaspoon cinnamon, remaining ¼ cup sugar and pecans; reserve topping for later use. Then bake as directed on next page.

Serve

warm or at room temperature with a dollop of whipped topping or scoop of ice cream.

COOK IT INSIDE

Oven — 10"

Preheat oven to 350°. Line bottom of Dutch oven with a circle of parchment paper. Lightly grease paper and sides of pot with nonstick cooking spray. Spread batter evenly in pot. Sprinkle reserved topping mixture over top, swirling into batter lightly with a knife, if desired. Bake for 35 to 40 minutes or until cake tests done with a toothpick. Let cool slightly before slicing.

COOK IT OUTSIDE

Campfire | **about 22 hot coals** — 10" w/lid

Line bottom of Dutch oven with a circle of parchment paper. Lightly grease paper and sides of pot with nonstick cooking spray. Spread batter evenly in pot. Sprinkle reserved topping mixture over top, swirling into batter lightly with a knife, if desired. Cover Dutch oven with lid.

Arrange about ⅓ of the hot coals in a cooking ring underneath Dutch oven. Place remaining hot coals on lid. Cook for 30 to 40 minutes or until cake tests done with a toothpick. Rotate pot and lid twice during cooking and adjust the number of coals on top and bottom as needed for even cooking.

Tip

For easy clean-up, line cookware with parchment paper or heavy-duty aluminum foil when cooking anything with sugar.

Apple Cake Dessert

Serves 8

2 eggs, lightly beaten	1 tsp. ground cinnamon
1 tsp. vanilla extract	½ tsp. ground nutmeg
½ C. melted butter	¼ tsp. ground cloves
1 C. flour	2 C. peeled, chopped apples
½ C. sugar	¼ C. chopped pecans
½ C. brown sugar	1 T. butter
¼ tsp. salt	Vanilla ice cream

BASIC DIRECTIONS

In a large bowl, whisk together eggs, vanilla and melted butter until smooth; set aside. In a medium bowl, stir together flour, sugar, brown sugar, salt, cinnamon, nutmeg and cloves to blend. Add apples and pecans to flour mixture and toss until coated. Stir apple mixture into egg mixture until thoroughly combined. Then cook as directed on next page.

Serve
warm with ice cream.

COOK IT INSIDE

8"-9"

Oven

Preheat oven to 350°. Place skillet in oven to preheat about 5 minutes. Remove from oven and add 1 tablespoon butter. When melted, swirl skillet to coat bottom and sides. Pour batter into hot skillet and spread evenly.

Return pan to oven and bake uncovered for 40 minutes or until lightly browned and cake tests done with a toothpick. Let cake cool in skillet about 20 minutes before slicing into wedges.

COOK IT OUTSIDE

10" w/lid

Campfire or Grill | about 22 hot coals

Arrange about ⅓ of the hot coals in a cooking ring underneath Dutch oven. Add 1 tablespoon butter; when melted, brush over bottom and sides of pot. Pour batter into hot pot and spread evenly. Cover with lid.

Place remaining hot coals on lid. Bake for 20 to 30 minutes or until lightly browned and cake tests done with a toothpick. Check cake after 15 minutes and rotate pot and lid. Adjust coals on top and bottom as needed for even cooking. When done, remove lid and let cake cool in skillet about 20 minutes before slicing into wedges.

Tip

Since cast iron retains heat so well, foods finish baking after being removed from heat. Avoid over-cooking baked goods.

Desserts

One-Pan Brownies

Serves 8

3 oz. unsweetened baking
    chocolate
¾ C. butter
½ C. sugar
1 C. brown sugar

3 eggs, lightly beaten
¾ C. flour
1 tsp. vanilla extract
Ice cream

BASIC DIRECTIONS

Leave chocolate pieces in wrappers and hit with a rolling pin several times to break chocolate into small chunks; set aside. Cut butter into pieces. Then proceed as directed on next page.

Serve
warm or at room temperature
with ice cream.

COOK IT INSIDE

10"

Stovetop & Oven

Preheat oven to 325°. Place skillet on stovetop over low heat and add chocolate pieces and butter. Cook and stir until melted and well blended.

Remove skillet from heat and stir in sugar and brown sugar until mixed. Whisk in eggs and vanilla. Add flour and whisk gently until all flour is incorporated. Scrape around sides of skillet and spread batter evenly.

Place skillet on center rack in oven and bake uncovered about 45 minutes or until brownies test done with a toothpick. Cool in skillet at least 15 minutes before cutting brownies into wedges.

COOK IT OUTSIDE

10"
w/lid

Campfire   18(+) hot coals

Arrange about ⅓ of the hot coals in a cooking ring underneath Dutch oven. Place chocolate pieces and butter in pot. Cook and stir until melted and well blended.

Remove Dutch oven from heat; stir in sugar and brown sugar until mixed. Whisk in eggs and vanilla. Add flour and whisk gently until all flour is incorporated. Scrape around sides of pot and spread batter evenly. Cover with lid.

Return Dutch oven to cooking ring and place remaining hot coals on lid. Cook for 30 to 40 minutes or until brownies test done with a toothpick. Rotate pot and lid several times during cooking and replenish coals on top and bottom as needed to maintain cooking temperature. Let cool at least 15 minutes before cutting brownies into wedges.

Easy Spiced Peach Cake

Serves 10

2 (21 oz.) cans
   peach pie filling
1 (18.25 oz.) pkg. spice
   cake mix

1 (12 oz.) can lemon-lime
   soda or ginger ale
   (not diet)
Vanilla ice cream, optional

BASIC DIRECTIONS

Lightly grease bottom of 12" Dutch oven with nonstick cooking spray. Spread both cans of pie filling evenly over bottom of pot. Sprinkle dry cake mix over fruit. Pour soda evenly over cake mix and swirl lightly with a fork several times to moisten and partially blend. Then cook as directed on next page.

Serve
   warm in bowls topped
   with ice cream, if desired.

COOK IT INSIDE

Oven

Preheat oven to 350°. Set Dutch oven on middle rack in oven and bake uncovered for 30 minutes or until bubbly around edges and cake is lightly browned on top and tests done with a toothpick. Let cool slightly before serving with a large spoon.

COOK IT OUTSIDE

Campfire **24 (+) hot coals**

Cover Dutch oven with lid. Arrange about ⅓ of the hot coals in a cooking ring underneath Dutch oven. Place remaining hot coals on lid. Cook for 30 to 40 minutes or until bubbly around edges and cake is lightly browned on top and tests done with a toothpick. Rotate pot and lid twice during cooking and replenish coals on top and bottom as needed to maintain cooking temperature. To promote browning on top, add several coals near handle on lid toward end of cooking time. Let cool slightly before serving with a large spoon.

Variations

- Soda may be replaced with ¾ cup melted butter.
- **Black Forest Cake:** use cherry pie filling, chocolate cake mix and cola
- **Apple Cake:** use apple pie filling, vanilla or spice cake mix and lemon-lime soda
- **Blueberry Cake:** use blueberry pie filling, vanilla cake mix and lemon-lime soda
- **Fruit Cobbler:** Prepare one (15 to 18 oz.) cake mix according to package directions. Pour batter over pie filling in Dutch oven, sprinkle with brown sugar and bake as directed.

Cherry Almond Cake

Serves 8

1 (10 oz.) jar maraschino cherries
½ tsp. vanilla extract
½ tsp. almond extract
2 C. flour
1 tsp. baking powder
½ tsp. salt
½ C. butter, softened

1 C. sugar
2 eggs
4 oz. white chocolate, chopped
½ C. sliced almonds
1 C. powdered sugar
Milk

BASIC DIRECTIONS

Drain cherries and reserve ½ cup juice in a measuring cup (add water if short). Add vanilla and almond extracts to juice. Cut cherries in half; set aside.

In a medium bowl, stir together flour, baking powder and salt. In a large mixing bowl, beat together butter and sugar until light and fluffy. Add eggs, one at a time, beating well after each addition. Add flour mixture and cherry juice alternately to creamed mixture in bowl, beating on low until well blended. Fold cherries into batter. Then proceed as directed on next page.

Serve
wedges at room temperature or warmed slightly.

COOK IT INSIDE

10"

Oven

Preheat oven to 350°. Grease skillet with nonstick cooking spray. Pour batter into skillet and sprinkle chopped chocolate over top. With a knife, gently swirl batter just to cover chocolate. Sprinkle with almonds. Bake uncovered for 1 hour or until cake tests done with a toothpick. Cool in pan for 15 minutes before inverting cake onto a wire rack to cool completely.

Meanwhile, in a small bowl, whisk together powdered sugar with enough milk to make a thin glaze. Drizzle glaze over cake before slicing into wedges.

COOK IT OUTSIDE

10" w/lid

Campfire   24 (+) hot coals

Grease Dutch oven with nonstick cooking spray. Line pot with parchment paper, if desired. Pour batter into pot and sprinkle chopped chocolate over top. With a knife, gently swirl batter just to cover chocolate. Sprinkle with almonds and cover pot with lid.

Arrange about ⅓ of the hot coals in a cooking ring underneath Dutch oven. Place remaining hot coals on lid. Cook for 50 to 60 minutes or until cake tests done with a toothpick. Rotate pot and lid several times during cooking and replenish coals on top and bottom as needed to maintain cooking temperature. Cool in pan for 15 minutes before inverting cake onto a wire rack to cool completely.

Meanwhile, in a small bowl, whisk together powdered sugar with enough milk to make a thin glaze. Drizzle glaze over cake before slicing into wedges.

Granny's Apple Pie

Serves 8

1 (14.1 oz.) pkg. refrigerated pie crust (2 ct.)

4 to 5 large apples (such as Granny Smith and/or Braeburn)

½ to ¾ C. sugar

2 T. brown sugar

1 tsp. ground cinnamon

⅛ tsp. ground nutmeg

2 T. flour

2 T. butter, cut into pieces

Egg white, optional

Coarse sugar, optional

Ice cream, optional

Caramel ice cream topping, optional

BASIC DIRECTIONS

Allow wrapped pie crusts to stand at room temperature for 15 minutes to soften. Peel and core apples; slice evenly. In a large bowl, mix sugar, brown sugar, cinnamon, nutmeg and flour; add apples and toss until coated. Then proceed as directed on next page.

Serve
pie wedges with ice cream and caramel topping, if desired.

COOK IT INSIDE

10"

Oven

Preheat oven to 350°. Unroll one pie crust and press over bottom and up sides of skillet. Spread prepared apple mixture over crust. Dot with pieces of butter. Unroll remaining pie crust and place over apples, crimping crust edges together. If desired, whisk egg white until frothy and brush over pie crust; sprinkle with coarse sugar. Cut several slits in top crust to vent steam. Place skillet on center rack in oven (with baking sheet underneath) and bake uncovered about 1 hour or until golden brown and bubbly. Shield edges with aluminum foil if necessary to prevent excess browning. Cool for 30 minutes before slicing.

COOK IT OUTSIDE

12" w/lid

Campfire   26 (+) hot coals

Unroll one pie crust and press over bottom and up sides of a 9" deep metal pie plate, allowing excess crust to hang over rim. Spread prepared apple mixture over crust. Dot with pieces of butter. Unroll remaining pie crust and place over apples. Overlap crust edges and crimp to seal. If desired, whisk egg white until frothy and brush over pie crust; sprinkle with coarse sugar. Cut several slits in top crust to vent steam.

Prepare riser in Dutch oven (figure 1 on page 54). Set pie plate on riser and cover pot with lid.

Arrange about ⅓ of the hot coals in a cooking ring under Dutch oven. Place remaining hot coals on lid. Cook for 50 to 60 minutes or until golden brown and bubbly. Rotate pot and lid several times during cooking and replenish coals on top and bottom as needed to maintain cooking temperature. To promote browning on top, add several hot coals near handle on lid toward end of cooking time. Cool for 30 minutes before slicing.

Nutty Hot Fudge Cake

Serves 10

1¼ C. sugar, divided
5 T. unsweetened cocoa powder, divided
½ C. brown sugar
1 C. flour
2 tsp. baking powder

¼ tsp. salt
½ C. milk
1 tsp. vanilla extract
2 T. butter, melted
¾ C. chopped pecans
Ice cream, optional

BASIC DIRECTIONS

In a small bowl, mix ½ cup sugar, 2 tablespoons cocoa powder and brown sugar; set topping aside. In a medium bowl, stir together flour, remaining ¾ cup sugar, baking powder, salt and remaining 3 tablespoons cocoa powder. Add milk and vanilla; stir until blended. Stir in melted butter and pecans. Then proceed as directed on next page.

Serve
warm or at room temperature with ice cream, if desired.

COOK IT INSIDE

Oven

10"

Preheat oven to 350°. Grease bottom of Dutch oven with nonstick cooking spray. Line pot with a circle of parchment paper, extending paper 2" up sides; spray paper. Spread batter in Dutch oven. Sprinkle set-aside topping over batter. Pour 1 cup boiling water over top of cake but do not stir.

Place Dutch oven on center rack in oven and bake uncovered for 30 to 35 minutes or until cake tests done with a toothpick.

Remove from oven and let stand 5 to 10 minutes. Carefully invert cake onto a lightly greased platter. Remove parchment paper and let cake cool at least 15 minutes before cutting.

COOK IT OUTSIDE

10" w/lid

Campfire | about 22 hot coals

Grease bottom of Dutch oven with nonstick cooking spray. Line pot with a circle of parchment paper, extending paper 2" up sides; spray paper. Spread batter in Dutch oven. Sprinkle set-aside topping over batter. Pour 1 cup boiling water over top of cake but do not stir. Cover Dutch oven.

Arrange about ⅓ of the hot coals in a cooking ring underneath Dutch oven. Place remaining hot coals on lid. Cook for 25 to 35 minutes or until cake tests done with a toothpick. Rotate pot and lid twice during cooking and adjust the number of coals on top and bottom as needed for even cooking.

Remove Dutch oven from heat and let stand about 5 minutes. Carefully invert cake onto a lightly greased platter. Remove parchment paper and let cake cool at least 15 minutes before cutting.

Banana Upside-Down Cake

Serves 8

5 fully ripe bananas, divided
½ C. buttermilk
1 tsp. vanilla extract
1½ C. flour
¾ tsp. baking soda
½ tsp. baking powder
½ tsp. salt
⅓ C. butter, softened

1¼ C. sugar
2 eggs
1 C. brown sugar
6 T. butter, melted
1 C. powdered sugar
Milk
Whipped topping, optional

BASIC DIRECTIONS

Peel and mash two bananas; measure 1 cup mashed fruit into a medium bowl. Add buttermilk and vanilla; stir well. In another bowl, whisk together flour, baking soda, baking powder and salt.

In a large mixing bowl, beat together softened butter and sugar until fluffy. Add eggs and beat well. Add dry ingredients and buttermilk mixture alternately to creamed mixture in bowl, beating until just combined. Then proceed as directed on next page.

Serve

warm or at room temperature
with whipped topping, if desired.

COOK IT INSIDE

10"

Oven

Preheat oven to 350°. Lightly grease Dutch oven and line with a circle of parchment paper, extending paper 2" up sides. Sprinkle brown sugar evenly over bottom of pot. Drizzle with melted butter. Peel and slice remaining three bananas and arrange slices in a single layer over brown sugar mixture. Spread prepared batter over banana slices.

Place Dutch oven on center rack in oven and bake for 35 to 40 minutes or until cake pulls away from side of pot and tests done with a toothpick. Let cake cool in Dutch oven for 20 minutes before carefully inverting onto a platter. Peel off parchment paper promptly.

In a small bowl, whisk together powdered sugar with enough milk to make a thin glaze. Drizzle over cake.

COOK IT OUTSIDE

10"
w/lid

Campfire   22 (+) hot coals

Lightly grease Dutch oven and line with a circle of parchment paper, extending paper 2" up sides. Sprinkle brown sugar evenly over bottom of pot. Drizzle with melted butter. Peel and slice remaining three bananas and arrange slices in a single layer over brown sugar mixture. Spread prepared batter over banana slices. Cover Dutch oven with lid.

Arrange about ⅓ of the hot coals in a cooking ring underneath Dutch oven. Place remaining hot coals on lid. Cook for 30 to 40 minutes or until cake is golden brown and tests done with a toothpick. Rotate pot and lid several times during cooking and replenish coals on top and bottom as needed to maintain cooking temperature. Let cake cool in Dutch oven for 20 minutes before carefully inverting onto a platter. Peel off parchment paper promptly.

In a small bowl, whisk together powdered sugar with enough milk to make a thin glaze. Drizzle over cake.

Berry Crumble

Serves 8

3 C. quick-cooking rolled oats

½ C. plus 2 T. whole wheat flour, divided

1 C. chopped pecans

1 C. brown sugar

1½ tsp. ground cinnamon

1 C. butter, cut into pieces

6 C. frozen berries (blueberries, raspberries, strawberries or any combination)

¼ C. sugar

Ice cream or sweetened whipped cream, optional

BASIC DIRECTIONS

In a large bowl, stir together oats, ½ cup flour, pecans, brown sugar and cinnamon. With a pastry blender or two knives, cut in butter until mixture is crumbly. Then proceed as directed on next page.

Serve

warm or at room temperature in bowls, topped with ice cream or whipped cream, if desired.

COOK IT INSIDE

12"

Oven

Preheat oven to 400°. Lightly grease skillet with nonstick cooking spray. Spread berries in pan. Sprinkle with sugar and remaining 2 tablespoons flour; toss gently to combine. Spread prepared oats mixture over top. Place on center rack in oven and bake about 30 minutes or until bubbly and golden brown. Let cool in skillet.

COOK IT OUTSIDE

12" w/lid

Campfire — about 30 hot coals

Lightly grease Dutch oven with nonstick cooking spray. Line pot with parchment paper, if desired. Spread berries in pot. Sprinkle with sugar and remaining 2 tablespoons flour; toss gently to combine. Spread prepared oats mixture over top and cover pot with lid.

Arrange about ⅓ of the hot coals in a cooking ring underneath Dutch oven. Place remaining hot coals on lid. Cook for 25 to 35 minutes or until bubbly and golden brown. Rotate pot and lid twice during cooking and adjust the number of coals on top and bottom as needed for even cooking. Remove lid and let cool in pot.

Variations

In place of berries, try fresh or frozen chopped rhubarb, peaches or apples. Thaw and drain frozen fruits before using.

Rhubarb Pie Dessert

Serves 10

2 eggs, beaten
1½ C. sugar
Dash of salt
1¼ C. flour, divided

3 C. chopped rhubarb*
⅓ C. powdered sugar
½ C. butter, cut into pieces

* If using frozen rhubarb, thaw and drain well before
combining with other ingredients, patting dry if necessary.

BASIC DIRECTIONS

In a large bowl, whisk together eggs, sugar, salt and ¼ cup flour until blended. Stir in rhubarb and reserve for later use.

In a medium bowl, combine remaining 1 cup flour, powdered sugar and butter. With pastry blender or two knives, cut in butter until crust mixture is crumbly. Then proceed as directed on next page.

Serve
wedges warm or at room temperature.

COOK IT INSIDE

10"

Oven

Preheat oven to 350°. Lightly grease skillet with nonstick cooking spray. Press prepared crust mixture into bottom of skillet and place in oven to bake for 12 minutes or until slightly browned.

Remove skillet from oven and let cool several minutes. Spread reserved rhubarb mixture evenly over warm crust. Return to oven and bake uncovered for 30 minutes more. Let cool at least 30 minutes before slicing and serving.

COOK IT OUTSIDE

10" w/lid

Campfire | about 24 hot coals

Lightly grease Dutch oven with nonstick cooking spray. Press crust mixture into bottom of pot and cover with lid.

Arrange about ⅓ of the hot coals in a cooking ring underneath Dutch oven. Place remaining hot coals on lid and bake crust for 10 to 15 minutes or until slightly browned.

Carefully remove lid. Spread prepared rhubarb mixture evenly over warm crust. Cover pot again and cook 25 to 35 minutes more. Rotate pot and lid twice during cooking and adjust the number of coals on top and bottom to reduce heat as needed to avoid overcooking. Let cool at least 30 minutes before slicing and serving.

Variations

In place of rhubarb, try fresh or canned peaches, pears or apples.

Jumbo Chipper Cookie

Serves 16

2¼ C. flour
1 tsp. baking soda
½ tsp. salt
½ C. vegetable shortening
½ C. butter, softened
¾ C. sugar
¾ C. brown sugar

2 tsp. vanilla extract
2 eggs
1 C. semi-sweet
   chocolate chips
1 C. butterscotch chips
Ice cream, optional

BASIC DIRECTIONS

In a medium bowl, whisk together flour, baking soda and salt. In a large mixing bowl, beat shortening and butter until creamy. Beat in sugar, brown sugar and vanilla. Add eggs and beat well. Gradually beat in dry ingredients until blended. Stir in chocolate and butterscotch chips. Then bake as directed on next page.

Serve
wedges alone or with ice cream.

COOK IT INSIDE

Oven

Preheat oven to 350°. Lightly grease skillet with nonstick cooking spray. Press prepared cookie dough evenly in bottom of skillet, flattening lightly. Bake about 30 minutes or until edges pull away from side of pan and top is golden brown. Remove from oven to a cooling rack and let cool in skillet for 15 minutes before removing from Dutch oven or cutting into wedges.

COOK IT OUTSIDE

12"
w/lid

Campfire   about 26 hot coals

Lightly grease Dutch oven with nonstick cooking spray. Press prepared cookie dough evenly in bottom of pot, flattening lightly. Cover pot with lid.

Arrange about ⅓ of the hot coals in a cooking ring underneath Dutch oven. Place remaining hot coals on lid. Cook for 25 to 35 minutes or until edges pull away from side of pot and top is golden brown. Rotate pot and lid several times during cooking and adjust the number of coals on top and bottom as needed for even browning. Uncover and let cool in skillet for 15 minutes before removing from pot or cutting into wedges.

Variations

Similar cookie recipes may be used following these cooking methods.

Tip

Rather than adding fresh coals near the end of cooking time, try brushing the ashes off existing coals so they'll burn hot for awhile longer.

Tips for Cast Iron Cookware

1. To build a good nonstick patina on new pans, cook foods with a high fat content the first few times you use them. For example, cooking bacon or sausage or frying chicken or donuts helps oil seep into the pores of cast iron.

2. After cooking soups, stews and other foods with a high water content, you may need to reseason your cookware.

3. Look inside your Dutch oven during cooking to monitor the heat and add or remove coals as needed to prevent under- or over-cooking. But try not to peek too often or too long, you'll release the heat needed for proper cooking.

4. Since campfire heat is somewhat irregular, check for doneness 5 to 10 minutes before the cooking time is up.

5. To increase browning on top during the last few minutes of baking, lift Dutch oven off bottom coals and transfer those coals to the lid.

6. If food is browning too quickly on the bottom, transfer some hot coals from bottom ring to lid or remove a few.

7. Cooking food with the lid on reduces cooking time.

8. If steam is escaping from under the lid on a Dutch oven, reduce the heat slightly.

9. Food can be cooked directly in a Dutch oven or in a secondary pan set on a "riser" inside so the Dutch oven acts like an oven. To make a "riser," place several metal nuts, clean pebbles, balls of foil or an inverted metal pie plate or canning jar ring inside the Dutch oven and set the baking pan of food on top. Cover pot with lid. (See figure 1 on page 54.)

10. When it is cold or windy outside, allow more time and coals for cooking.

11. If it's hot and sunny outside, charcoal briquettes generate more heat and you may need to reduce cooking time.

12. Use a clean paintbrush to brush ashes off the lid of a Dutch oven.

Index of Recipes

Breakfast

Breads

Main Dishes

Side Dishes

Desserts